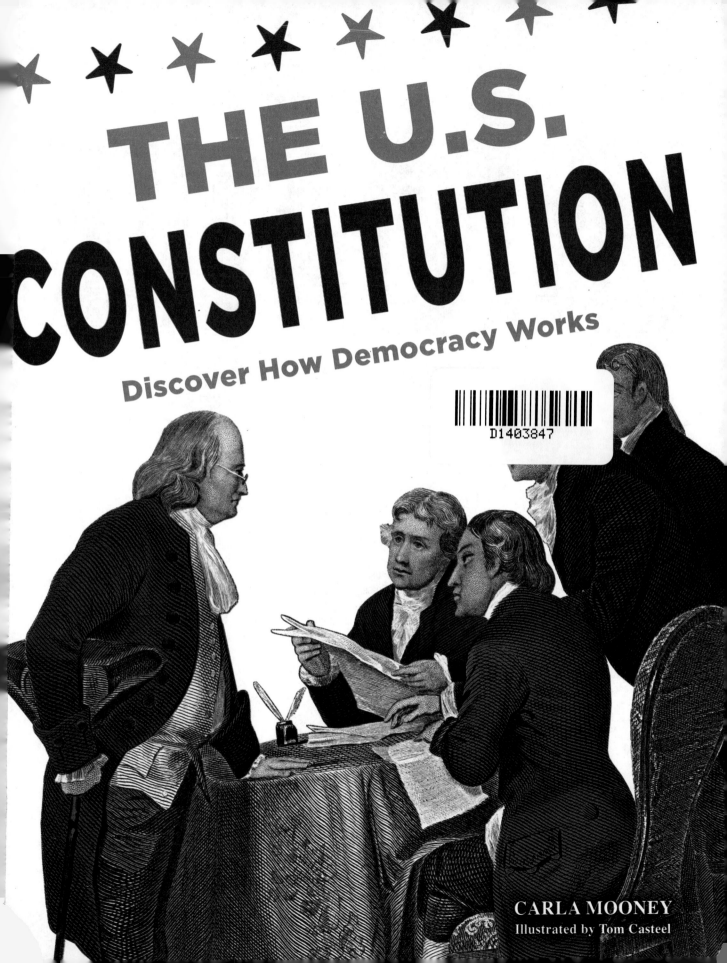

THE U.S. CONSTITUTION

Discover How Democracy Works

D1403847

CARLA MOONEY

Illustrated by Tom Casteel

~ More U.S. history titles in the *Build It Yourself* Series ~

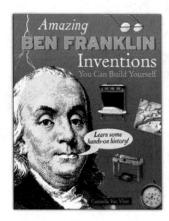 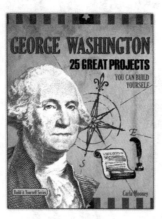 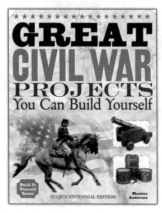 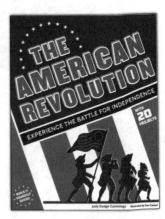

Check out more titles at www.nomadpress.net

Nomad Press
A division of Nomad Communications
10 9 8 7 6 5 4 3 2 1

This book was manufactured by Marquis Book Printing,
Louiseville, Québec, Canada
September 2016, Job #125550

ISBN Softcover: 978-1-61930-445-1
ISBN Hardcover: 978-1-61930-441-3

Educational Consultant, Marla Conn

Questions regarding the ordering of this book should be addressed to
Nomad Press
2456 Christian St.
White River Junction, VT 05001
www.nomadpress.net

Printed in Canada.

CONTENTS

Water damaged prior 6/29/18 JR

Interested in Primary Sources?

Look for this icon. Use a smartphone or tablet app to scan the QR code and explore more about the U.S. Constitution and other documents! You can find a list of URLs on the Resources page.

If the QR code doesn't work, try searching the Internet with the Keyword Prompts to find other helpful sources.

U.S. Constitution 🔎

Fifth century BCE: The city–state of Athens in ancient Greece establishes one of the first known direct democracies.

1215: Britain's King John places his seal on Magna Carta.

1600–1800: A period called the Enlightenment occurs in Europe. This is a movement that emphasizes reason and individualism.

1619: The Virginia House of Burgesses is the first representative legislative body in the Americas.

1620: The Mayflower Compact, signed by the Pilgrims, forms a government based on majority rule.

1689: England's Parliament passes the English Bill of Rights. It creates a constitutional monarchy and limits the power of the king.

1765: The British Parliament passes the Stamp Act and imposes a new tax, on paper, on the American colonists.

1773: Anger over a British tax on tea leads to the Boston Tea Party, when a group of colonists dump tea from British ships into Boston Harbor.

March 1774: Parliament passes the Coercive Acts, a series of laws that close Boston's port and deny colonists in Massachusetts the right to elect their officials.

September–October 1774: Delegates from every colony except Georgia meet in Philadelphia at the First Continental Congress.

May 1775: Delegates from all 13 colonies meet in Philadelphia at the Second Continental Congress. They send the Olive Branch Petition to King George III.

July 1775: The Second Continental Congress issues the Declaration of Arms.

January 1776: Thomas Paine publishes his pamphlet, *Common Sense.*

June 1776: Virginia approves the Virginia Declaration of Rights and calls for independence from Great Britain.

July 1776: The Second Continental Congress approves the Declaration of Independence.

1777: The Second Continental Congress approves the Articles of Confederation.

September 1783: The Treaty of Paris is signed between the United States of America and England, formally ending the Revolutionary War.

1787: The Constitutional Convention convenes in Philadelphia to discuss revising the Articles of Confederation. Eventually, the delegates write an entirely new document, the United States Constitution. All state delegations, except Rhode Island, approve the Constitution.

October 1787: A series of articles supporting ratification of the Constitution appear in the New York press. They become known as the Federalist Papers.

December 1787: Delaware becomes the first state to ratify the Constitution.

1788: The Constitution becomes effective when New Hampshire becomes the ninth state to ratify it.

1789: The first Congress under the Constitution meets in New York City.

April 1789: George Washington is elected the first president of the United States under the Constitution with 69 electoral votes. John Adams is elected vice president with 34 votes.

June 1789: James Madison introduces the proposed Bill of Rights in the House of Representatives.

August 1789: The French people rebel against their monarchy and adopt the French Declaration of the Rights of Man and of the Citizen.

September 1789: Congress establishes a Supreme Court, 13 district courts, three circuit courts, and the position of attorney general.

September 1789: Congress approves 12 amendments to the Constitution and sends them to the states for ratification.

November 1789: New Jersey is the first state to ratify the Bill of Rights.

February 1790: The Supreme Court convenes for the first time.

May 1790: Rhode Island is the last state to ratify the Constitution.

1791: The first 10 amendments to the Constitution, known as the Bill of Rights, are ratified.

1848: The Declaration of Sentiments calling for women's rights is issued at the Seneca Falls Convention.

January 1863: President Abraham Lincoln issues the Emancipation Proclamation, freeing all slaves held in the Confederate states outside of Union control.

November 1863: President Lincoln gives the Gettysburg Address at a cemetery dedication ceremony in Pennsylvania.

1865: The Thirteenth Amendment to abolish slavery is ratified.

1868: The Fourteenth Amendment is ratified, granting citizenship to all people born in the United States and guaranteeing due process and equal protection to all people, including former slaves and their descendants.

1870: The Fifteenth Amendment is ratified, prohibiting states from denying voting rights to citizens based on race or color.

1900: About 10 democracies exist worldwide.

1920: The Nineteenth Amendment is ratified, prohibiting states from denying voting rights based on sex.

1948: The United Nations adopts the Universal Declaration of Human Rights.

1954: In Brown v. Board of Education, the U.S. Supreme Court rules that separate public schools for black and white students is unconstitutional.

1964: Congress passes the Civil Rights Act.

1965: Congress passes the Voting Rights Act.

2008: Barack Obama successfully uses social media in his campaign for president.

2011: The Occupy Movement uses the Internet and social media to organize and stage protests over social and economic inequalities around the world.

2016: The White House issues videos on YouTube to connect with the people of the United States.

2016: More than 100 democracies exist worldwide and most of them have a written constitution.

WHAT IS DEMOCRACY?

"Life, **liberty** and the pursuit of happiness"—these stirring words from the Declaration of Independence have been quoted for hundreds of years as three rights of all citizens of the United States.

Americans are known for fiercely protecting these rights and speaking out against injustice. Where did this expectation of rights come from? How does the American government protect these rights? By closely reading documents that were crafted hundreds of years ago, such as the U.S. Constitution, we find the answers to these questions and discover how American democracy works.

liberty: social and political freedoms enjoyed by people.

democracy: a system of government where the people have the ultimate power to govern themselves and determine how they will be governed.

representative democracy: a form of democracy where elected officials govern.

polls: a survey (or count) of people's positions on issues or candidates for elected office, or a place where that survey (or count) takes place.

civic: relating to duty and responsibility to community.

human rights: the rights that belong to all people, such as freedom from torture, the right to live, and freedom from slavery.

citizen: a person who has all the rights and responsibilities that come with being a full member of a country.

direct democracy: a form of democracy where all citizens participate in decision making.

WORDS TO KNOW

WHAT IS A DEMOCRACY?

A **democracy** is a system of government. In fact, a democracy is the most common form of government in the world. The word *democracy* comes from two Greek words—*demos*, which means "people," and *cracy*, which means "rule of."

Democracy is a form of government that gives power to the people. In the United States, the U.S. Constitution is the document that defines that power and the way the government is structured. Our constitutional democracy has four key elements.

• A political system that allows the people to choose and replace government officials through free and fair elections. This is **representative democracy**. Have you ever gone to the **polls** with an adult on election day? You witnessed representational democracy in action!

• Citizens who actively participate in politics and **civic** life.

• Protection of the **human rights** of all people, not just its **citizens** and not just certain groups.

• A government that is based on the rule of law and limited by those laws, where the laws apply equally to all.

Democracies can be direct or representative. In a **direct democracy**, all citizens participate in making public decisions, without elected or appointed officials. A direct democracy works best with small numbers of people. Is there a neighborhood organization where you live? It might operate as a direct democracy. In small groups, members can meet in one place to discuss issues and make decisions by a majority vote.

The world's first democracy, Athens in ancient Greece, was a direct democracy. Assemblies with as many as 5,000 to 6,000 people gathered to practice direct democracy.

What would it look like if every citizen of the United States had to meet every time a law needed to be voted on?

In many communities, the population is too large or spread out for all to gather in a single location to vote or discuss issues. As a result, the most common form of democracy is a representative democracy.

In this form of democracy, the people elect officials to make political decisions, create laws, and administer public programs for them. This group of officials is a manageable size that meets to discuss issues in depth before they vote. They hold office in the name of the people. If the people are not satisfied with their elected officials, they can vote them out of office and replace them with new officials.

BCE: put after a date, BCE stands for Before Common Era and counts down to zero. CE stands for Common Era and counts up from zero. These nonreligious terms correspond to BC and AD. This book was printed in 2016 CE.

lottery: a random selection.

jury: a group of people, called jurors, who hear a case in court. Jurors give their opinion, called a verdict.

Middle Ages: the name for a period of time from around 350 to 1450 CE. It is also called the Medieval Era.

noble: in the past, a person considered to be of the most important group in a society.

legislative: having to do with the branch of government that makes or changes laws.

reason: thinking in an orderly, sensible way.

individualism: the pursuit of personal happiness and independence rather than the goals or interests of a group.

philosopher: a person who thinks about and questions the way things are in the world and in the universe.

WORDS TO KNOW

A HISTORY OF DEMOCRACY

Democracy began long before the United States was a country. It's useful to learn about the history of democracy to understand how the system works today.

The city–state of Athens in ancient Greece, which existed around the fifth and sixth centuries **BCE**, was one of the first known direct democracies. The main political institution in Athens was called the Assembly. A ruling council of 500 citizens were chosen by **lottery** and served a one-year term. The council proposed policies that were voted on by the citizens of Athens. The Assembly conducted trials in which **juries** decided guilt or innocence by a majority vote.

In ancient Greece, membership in the Assembly and voting rights were limited to adult men.

Women, slaves, and foreigners were not allowed to vote. In some Greek city–states, only male property owners were eligible to vote. In this way, the early Greek model was a limited democracy, because not all of the people could participate. Still, the Greek city–states served as models for future democracies.

The **Middle Ages** began a period in which most European countries were ruled by a king or queen. Many people believed that the power of the king came directly from God!

In towns and villages, European communities often practiced limited democracy. The people elected town leaders and representatives. In some countries, the kings relied on assemblies of **nobles** for advice. These assemblies were similar to the modern **legislative** assemblies we have today. For example, in 1295, England's King Edward I called together all the nobles, along with several important middle-class citizens and officials, to discuss political matters. These meetings were an early version of the English Parliament, the legislative body in England today.

Between 1600 and 1800, Europe entered a period of time called the Age of Enlightenment. This movement emphasized **reason** and **individualism**. During this time, some **philosophers** argued for full democracy. French philosopher Jean-Jacques Rousseau (1712–1778) said that government existed with the consent of the people and that all citizens should have a role in politics.

DID YOU KNOW?

The word *parliament* comes from the French work *parler*, which means "to talk."

Man or Slave?

Jean-Jacques Rousseau was a philosopher, writer, and composer who greatly influenced the Age of Enlightenment. Read the following quote from his book, *The Social Contract*. What do you think it means? Rewrite it in your own words.

"Man was born free and everywhere he is in chains. One man thinks himself the master of others, but remains more of a slave than they . . . Any law that is made without the people voting for it is not a law at all."

Protestant Reformation: a religious movement beginning in 1500 that rejected the Catholic pope and established the Protestant churches.

elite: those viewed as the most important people.

autocracy: a form of government in which one person possesses unlimited power.

dictatorship: a government by a dictator with absolute rule over the people.

monarchy: a form of government where all power is given to a single individual, a king or queen.

constitution: a document containing a country's basic laws and governing principles.

WORDS TO KNOW

At about the same time, the **Protestant Reformation** (1500–1650) spread across Europe. Reformation leaders argued against the belief that kings had the divine right to rule from God. They called for a separation between church and government.

During these years, a growing number of European officials began to support democracy. In England, Parliament began to take on a more important role in government. In 1689, the English Bill of Rights gave Parliament a permanent role in the government. Although at the time Parliament was open only to the wealthy and **elite**, its actions laid the foundation for future democracies.

～～～～ TYPES OF GOVERNMENT ～～～～

While democracy is the most popular form of government, there are several other types of government in countries around the world. These countries often have documents that reflect the different types of governments. Governments can be defined by answering this question: Who rules? Some governments are ruled by a single individual, while others are ruled by the people.

DID YOU KNOW?

Today, some countries, such as England and Sweden, still have a king or queen, but they no longer have complete control over the country or its people. Instead, the monarch shares power with other government bodies.

Rule by One: An **autocracy** is a type of government that is ruled by one person who has total control. It is the oldest form of government. In an autocracy, control is usually kept by military or police power.

There are two main types of autocracy: a **dictatorship** and a **monarchy**. In a dictatorship, a ruler called a dictator gains power through force. The people must follow the dictator's policies whether or not they agree with them. If there is a **constitution**, the dictator controls it. Courts or other lawmaking bodies are also controlled by the dictator. In the 1930s and 1940s, Germany was under control of the dictator Adolf Hitler.

In a monarchy, a king or queen rules the country for their lifetime. Upon their death or retirement, they pass the crown to the next person in their family, usually a first-born child. In the past, many monarchs had absolute power. They owned all of the public land and claimed to be representatives of God on earth. England, France, and Sweden were all once ruled by monarchies.

theocracy: government rule by religious leaders.

deity: a god or goddess.

oligarchy: government rule by a small group.

communist party: a political party that follows a system in which everything is owned and run by the government.

totalitarian: a system of government that has absolute control over its people and requires them to be completely obedient.

propaganda: ideas or statements that are sometimes exaggerated or even false. They are spread to help a cause, political leader, or government.

republic: a form of democracy, with elected officials.

anarchy: a society without a government.

WORDS TO KNOW

Rule by Religion: In a **theocracy**, government leaders are usually priests or ministers who rule in the name of God or another **deity**. The Greek word *theos* means "god." The country's laws are based on religious laws. A theocracy can also be a democracy, dictatorship, monarchy, or other kind of government. In a theocracy, a large number of the people have the same religion. The people believe that their religious and political leaders have been chosen by God. Today, many Middle Eastern countries, such as Saudi Arabia, are Islamic theocracies. Vatican City is a Christian theocracy with the pope as its leader.

Rule by a Few: When a small group of people holds all the power, the government is an **oligarchy**. The word *oligarchy* comes from a Greek word that means "rule by a few." In some oligarchies, only one group has political rights. This group might be members of a particular political party, social class, or race. The former Soviet Union was an example of an oligarchy. It was ruled by the Politburo, the central committee of the **Communist Party**. The members of the Politburo had lots of political power.

DID YOU KNOW?

A plutocracy is government by the wealthy, whose power comes from their wealth. Can you think of any governments that are plutocracies or are becoming plutocracies?

An oligarchy can be **totalitarian**. This form of government maintains total control over citizens, including all parts of their public and private lives. Totalitarianism is like a dictatorship by a political party instead of by a single person. The rulers do not allow anyone else to form a political party. They have complete control over the military, economy, and all forms of communication, including newspapers, radio, television, and **propaganda**.

Rule by the People: Some governments give power to the citizens. Democracies are examples of rule by the people. A **republic** is a democratic model where the people elect officials to government office. The president is elected by the people to head the government.

In a republic, citizens do not govern the country themselves, but do it through elected representatives. A republic can describe any form of government in which the elected head of state is not a monarch who inherited the role. Citizens still hold the power in a republic, because if they do not like what their elected representatives are doing, they can vote them out of office.

No Government At All

Some countries that are in the middle of a war or a period of civic unrest have no functioning government. These countries are in a state of **anarchy**. Anarchists are people who believe that everyone should be free to live without being subject to any government.

THE U.S. CONSTITUTION AND ~~~ DOCUMENTS OF DEMOCRACY ~~~

Soon after the Revolutionary War, at the birth of the United States, the Founding Fathers created the U.S. Constitution. This is the most important document in American history! The Constitution affects each citizen, every day.

In this book, you will explore what the Founding Fathers were thinking when they wrote the Constitution and how their words are interpreted and applied today. We will explore other documents of American democracy, including the Articles of Confederation, the Declaration of Independence, and the Bill of Rights, to gain a better understanding of how our democracy works. We will compare and contrast these documents to the important documents of other nations, including Magna Carta and the French Rights of Man.

Are you ready to use documents of the past to learn how democracy works today?

Good Study Practices

Every good historian keeps a history journal! As you read through this book and do the activities, keep track of your ideas and observations and record them in your history journal.

Each chapter of this book begins with an essential question to help guide your exploration of U.S. history. Keep the question in your mind as you read the chapter. At the end of each chapter, use your history journal to record your thoughts and answers.

?

ESSENTIAL QUESTION

How does democracy differ from other forms of government?

Explore Different Types of Government

Every form of government has key features and characteristics that define it. For example, in a democracy, the citizens have a voice in laws and policies, but in a totalitarian country, the rulers make all decisions about public and private life. In this activity, you will explore how different forms of government would impact your classroom or family.

With a group of friends or other students, divide into several groups and decide on a form of government for each group—democracy, monarchy, dictatorship, and oligarchy. Design sets of rules according to that system.

* How will each group operate? What are the key features of each type of government?

* How do these features appear in the group's rules?

* What are the benefits and drawbacks of each type of government?

* Did any form of government feel more fair than the others? Did any feel unfair?

* How are people in the group able to object to the things they find unfair?

Hold an imaginary summit meeting among all the government types to discuss a contemporary issue, such as climate change or immigration.

* What kinds of ideas might each group have?

* What kind of guidelines might the groups have to establish to be productive?

* Does each group's thoughts about the issues reflect the way their government is structured?

FIRST DOCUMENTS

In the mid-1700s, the American **colonies** stretched along the eastern coast of North America, from present-day Maine as far south as Georgia. The colonists were British subjects. They were loyal to Britain's newly crowned king, King George III. As British subjects, the colonists were ruled by Magna Carta. This thirteenth-century English document established that no one, not even the king, was above the law. Under Magna Carta, no one could take away certain rights of British citizens.

Although they remained under British rule, the American colonies were thousands of miles from Great Britain. British rulers had little interest in colonial affairs. By 1765, American colonists had handled things on their own for nearly 150 years.

? ESSENTIAL QUESTION

How did the Declaration of Independence lead to the Revolutionary War?

The colonists elected members to **legislatures** and passed local laws. They paid taxes to support colonial governments and **militias**. Colonial shippers and merchants still paid some taxes to Britain on imported goods. However, there came a time when King George decided these taxes weren't enough.

colony: an area that is controlled by or belongs to another country.

legislature: the lawmaking body of a government.

militia: a group of citizens who have been trained to fight and can be called upon when needed.

WORDS TO KNOW

NEW TAXES

In 1765, King George had a lot of bills to pay. The Seven Years' War (1755–1764) between England and France had been long and expensive. In North America, the French and Indian War (1754–1763) added to the debts that Britain owed. After the war, Britain kept soldiers in the colonies to protect the frontier to the west of the colonies.

The Mayflower Compact

The Mayflower Compact was written by the settlers arriving at New Plymouth after crossing the Atlantic Ocean aboard the *Mayflower*. It is the first governing document of Plymouth Colony. Earlier New World settlements had failed because of a lack of government. The pilgrims created the compact to ensure their own survival. It was signed on the ship in 1620 by all of the 41 adult male passengers. The Mayflower Compact became the first example of written laws in the New World. The original document has been lost, but you can read a page of it that was found in Governor William Bradford's history of the settlement at Plymouth.

Mayflower Compact 🔍

WORDS TO KNOW

boycott: refusing to buy or sell goods as part of a protest.

resolution: a formal declaration of a political position or principle.

delegate: a person sent to represent others.

King George III and his ministers decided that the American colonists should help pay some of these bills. The colonists disagreed. They believed that the war had not been fought to protect them, but to protect British trade interests in the colonies.

In 1765, the British Parliament passed the Stamp Act. The act was a new tax on all American colonists. It required them to pay a tax on every piece of printed paper they used. Ship's papers, legal documents, newspapers, and even playing cards were taxed.

The colonists protested the Stamp Act immediately. Until now, colonial assemblies and legislatures had made decisions about important taxes for the colonies.

For the first time, England was trying to tax the colonists directly.

The Stamp Act highlighted a basic disagreement between England and the colonies. The colonists believed that, as British citizens, they had the right to be taxed only by representatives that they had elected. Yet there were no American representatives in Parliament. Therefore, the colonists argued that the Stamp Act went directly against their basic right of no taxation without representation.

In addition, the colonists feared this tax would open the door to more taxes in the future. Parliament, however, believed that it had complete power over the colonies, including the right to tax them.

PROTEST!

Protests against the Stamp Act spread throughout the colonies. In Boston, mobs attacked the homes of wealthy tax collectors and the governor, Thomas Hutchinson. Merchants protested the Stamp Act by **boycotting** British goods. In Virginia, a young lawyer named Patrick Henry proposed several **resolutions** against the Stamp Act.

The dispute over the Stamp Act brought the colonists together against Great Britain for the first time. In October 1765, **delegates** from nine colonies met in New York City. They sent a petition to King George asking him to recognize their rights under British law.

Many British citizens were surprised at the colonists' opposition to the Stamp Act. They believed that Parliament had the right to tax the colonists.

rebel: to oppose. Rebels are people who stand up to oppose a ruler or government.

WORDS TO KNOW

The British merchants were upset over the colonists' boycott of their goods. They pressured Parliament to repeal the act. In 1766, Parliament did repeal the Stamp Act. But at the same time, it passed the Declaratory Act, which stated that Parliament had the right to rule and tax the colonies.

TENSIONS RISE

During the next few years, conflicts between England and the colonies continued. In 1767, Parliament passed another set of laws called the Townshend Acts, which put taxes on paint, glass, lead, paper, and tea imported into America. Again, the colonists **rebelled**

with protests, boycotts, and speeches against the acts. In 1773, tensions rose further when ships loaded with British tea arrived in Boston Harbor. Colonists disguised as Native Americans boarded the ships and dumped the tea into the harbor, an event known as the Boston Tea Party.

In London, the British government reacted immediately. It wanted the colonists punished for destroying British property. Parliament passed the Coercive Acts in 1774, which were a series of laws relating to the colonies that closed Boston's port and denied the people of Massachusetts the right to elect their officials. British troops now occupied Boston.

Outrage spread throughout the colonies. They called the new laws the "Intolerable Acts." In 1774, delegates from every colony except Georgia met in Philadelphia at the First Continental Congress. The delegates agreed to boycott British goods. They urged each colony to arm and train a militia so that the colonies could defend themselves against the British if needed.

The Continental Congress appealed to the king to make peace with the colonies. But peace did not come. Instead, armed conflict between British soldiers and the Massachusetts militia broke out in Lexington and Concord, Massachusetts, in April 1775. The American Revolution had begun.

～ SECOND CONTINENTAL CONGRESS ～

In May 1775, delegates from all 13 colonies met in Philadelphia at the Second Continental Congress. They appointed George Washington, a veteran of the French and Indian War, to build and lead a Continental Army.

At the same time, many still hoped war could be avoided. They wanted to remain part of Great Britain, but they also wanted to rule themselves through their own legislatures and elected officials. They sent King George III the Olive Branch Petition, asking him to stop the war and make peace with the colonies. But the king declared the colonists to be rebels. He sent more troops to the colonies. This reaction, along with the continued fighting between the colonists and British soldiers, led more Americans to think that independence was the only solution.

authority: the power or right to give orders, make decisions, and enforce the laws.

blockade: the sealing off of a place to prevent people and goods from entering or leaving.

mercenary: a hired soldier.

WORDS TO KNOW

~ *COMMON SENSE* ~

In January 1776, an English-American writer named Thomas Paine published a pamphlet titled *Common Sense*. It was the first written document that openly called for independence from Great Britain.

In this work, Paine argued that American colonists should challenge the **authority** of the British government and its monarchy. He argued that Great Britain provided few benefits to the colonies and only wanted to exploit them. Paine wrote his arguments in plain language that everyone could understand. Within a few months, *Common Sense* sold more than 500,000 copies. People passed it around and read it aloud.

At the time, many people were undecided about independence. Some still wanted to reconcile with Great Britain. When they read *Common Sense*, however, many people changed their minds and began to lean toward independence.

Olive Branch Petition

Drafted on July 5, 1775, the Olive Branch Petition was a letter from the members of the Second Continental Congress to King George III. In the letter, the colonists stated that they were loyal to Great Britain and asked the king to prevent further conflict. However, the king refused to receive the petition. You can see and read the original copy of the Olive Branch Petition at this website. How do you think your life would be different if King George III had responded differently to this document?

Olive Branch Petition archives 🔍

～ THE DECLARATION OF INDEPENDENCE ～

After *Common Sense* was published, Congress debated what to do. Should they try to make peace with Great Britain? Should they declare independence? Delegates fiercely argued the issue. Then, during the winter, Parliament ordered a **blockade** of all American trade, another move that angered the colonists. Rumors swirled that King George III had hired German **mercenaries** to fight against the colonists. The people were outraged that the king would hire foreign soldiers to fight against his own subjects!

DID YOU KNOW?

The Declaration of Arms was a statement issued by the Second Continental Congress in July 1775 in response to the fighting between the colonists and British soldiers at Lexington, Concord, and Bunker Hill. In the Declaration of Arms, the Congress listed the causes and reasons for the colonists taking up arms, but did not yet declare independence.

By spring 1776, Americans in town meetings and assemblies began to vote for independence from Great Britain. They sent the results of the votes to their delegates at the Second Continental Congress in Philadelphia. There, the fierce debate continued.

In early June 1776, Richard Henry Lee of Virginia presented a resolution approved by the Virginia legislature that called for dissolving the ties between the colonies and Great Britain. Seven states supported the resolution for independence. Six did not, including Pennsylvania, New York, New Jersey, Maryland, Delaware, and South Carolina. A final vote was scheduled in three weeks.

In the meantime, Congress appointed a committee to write a formal declaration of independence.

DID YOU KNOW?

The first time the formal term "The United States of America" was used was in the Declaration of Independence.

They chose five men—Benjamin Franklin, Thomas Jefferson, Robert Livingston, Roger Sherman, and John Adams. The committee agreed on what should be included in the document. Then they chose Thomas Jefferson, a young lawyer from Virginia, to write it. For about two weeks, Jefferson labored over the document in a second-floor room in a bricklayer's house in Philadelphia. When he finished, he gave it to Benjamin Franklin and John Adams, who made a few changes. Then they submitted the document to Congress.

The Declaration of Independence

The first two paragraphs of the Declaration of Independence state the following.

"When in the Course of human events, it becomes necessary for one people to dissolve the political bands which have connected them with another, and to assume among the powers of the earth, the separate and equal station to which the Laws of Nature and of Nature's God entitle them, a decent respect to the opinions of mankind requires that they should declare the causes which impel them to the separation.

*"We hold these truths to be self-evident, that all men are created equal, that they are endowed by their Creator with certain **unalienable** Rights, that among these are Life, Liberty and the pursuit of Happiness. —That to secure these rights, Governments are instituted among Men, deriving their just powers from the consent of the governed, —That whenever any Form of Government becomes destructive of these ends, it is the Right of the People to alter or to **abolish** it, and to institute new Government, laying its foundation on such **principles** and organizing its powers in such form, as to them shall seem most likely to effect their Safety and Happiness."*

You can read the rest of the document at this website.
How does this document affect your own life?

Declaration of Independence 🔍

On July 2, 1776, the Continental Congress voted to adopt Richard Henry Lee's resolution for independence. Two days later, on July 4, 1776, they officially approved the Declaration of Independence. Printed copies were sent to state assemblies, conventions, and the commanding officers of the Continental Army. On July 19, Congress ordered that the Declaration be **engrossed** on parchment. On August 2, 1776, John Hancock, the president of the Congress, signed the Declaration of Independence. The other delegates followed, each adding his signature to the document.

treason: actions that go against one's own country.

justify: to show that something is right and reasonable.

preamble: a brief, introductory statement.

reform: a change to improve something.

quarter: to provide lodging and food for soldiers.

WORDS TO KNOW

The delegates to the Continental Congress knew that signing the document would be considered **treason** by the British government. Each man risked his life and the lives of his family members by signing the parchment. They did it because they believed firmly in the cause of independence.

The Declaration of Independence announced to the world that the 13 American colonies were separating from Great Britain and forming the United States of America. It explained why the colonies were claiming independence and included a long list of charges against King George III. The document **justified** the American Revolution in words that have inspired people to stand up for their rights ever since.

DID YOU KNOW?
On July 8, 1776, Colonel John Nixon gave the first public reading of the Declaration of Independence at Independence Square in Philadelphia.

∼ WHAT DID IT SAY? ∼

Jefferson organized the Declaration of Independence into three main sections— the introduction, a list of wrongs committed by the king, and a conclusion. The first paragraphs of the introduction, known as the **preamble**, explain why the document is needed and why the colonies decided to separate themselves from Great Britain. In the second paragraph, Jefferson declared that "all men are created equal." He argued that people have certain rights that governments should not violate. These rights include the right to life, liberty, and the pursuit of happiness.

Jefferson further explained that when a government failed to protect these basic human rights, the people had a duty to **reform** the government or even overthrow it, if necessary. These ideas would be expressed again in the Constitution and form the basis of our beliefs about the role of government in the United States.

In the longest section of the document, Jefferson listed 27 charges against the king. He charged that the king had passed laws that affected the colonies without their approval. These laws included taxes on the colonists. Some laws forced them to **quarter** British soldiers. Others removed the colonists' right to trial by jury and blocked free trade. In addition, the Declaration of Independence charged that the king had authorized

violence against the colonies and did not let them govern themselves. By listing these charges, the document explained to the world why the Americans believed they were justified in their revolution.

In the conclusion, the Declaration of Independence named the 13 colonies as "the united States of America." By capitalizing "State," the writers showed that the 13 states would remain separate from each other, even though they were joined together for independence. The Declaration of Independence then formally declared independence.

The new nation claimed the rights of an independent country, such as the ability to engage in war, conduct trade, and make alliances.

ratify: to approve formally.

minority: a number or amount that is less than half of the whole.

majority: a number or amount that is greater than half of the whole.

sovereign: having supreme or ultimate power.

treaty: an agreement between countries or parties.

executive branch: the person or branch of government that enforces the law.

judicial branch: the branch of government that interprets the law.

WORDS TO KNOW

ARTICLES OF CONFEDERATION

With the Declaration of Independence, the colonists declared independence from Great Britain. But the new country did not have a central government in place.

With the Revolutionary War raging, the Second Continental Congress quickly worked to design a new government that could lead the people through the trials of war and beyond. At the same time, Congress urged each state to draft its own state constitution.

The Articles of Confederation and Perpetual Union was drafted by the Second Continental Congress in 1776. It was approved by the Congress in November 1777. After it was **ratified** by all 13 states on March 1, 1781, the articles became the new country's first constitution. The Articles of Confederation marked the first step for the 13 American colonies toward becoming a unified nation.

Minority and Majority

Take a look at your classroom or your family. How many girls are there? How many boys? Unless there is an equal number, one of those will be the **minority** and the other will be the **majority**. In a democracy, whoever wins more than half of the votes, or the majority, is the winner. However, a minority that expresses itself using the tools protected under the U.S. Constitution, such as the freedom of speech, is still a powerful force and can affect change.

The Articles of Confederation established a loose union among the 13 American states. Congress was hesitant to create a central government with too much power. Therefore, the Articles of Confederation left most power with the individual states. The states were **sovereign** and independent.

Under the articles, the central government had a single branch, a national legislature. This legislature was made up of representatives from each state and was given limited powers. It could conduct foreign affairs, make **treaties** and alliances, and declare war and peace. It could maintain an army and a navy and could coin money. The legislature would also act to resolve disputes between the states. However, Congress did not have the power to collect taxes, regulate trade between the states, or enforce laws. There was no **executive** or **judicial branch** of the central government.

NEW JERSEY DELAWARE

The Articles of Confederation did not work well. Instead of working together as a single nation, each state acted alone in its best interest. Each state had different trading policies and even different currencies. The central government was too weak to be effective. It could not pay for a strong military. And it could not raise the money needed to pay debts from the Revolutionary War.

Within a few years, the nation's leaders realized they needed to make a change. In 1787, a convention was called to rewrite the Articles of Confederation. Once the convention began, the delegates decided that an entirely new document was needed in order to bring the states together as a nation.

? ■ ESSENTIAL QUESTION

Now it's time to consider and discuss the Essential Question: How did the Declaration of Independence lead to the Revolutionary War?

How Did the Virginia Declaration of Rights Influence Thomas Jefferson?

In May 1776, the Virginia Convention met in Williamsburg, Virginia. The convention was a political meeting. On May 15, 1776, the convention declared independence from Great Britain. It called for a declaration of rights for Virginia. Members of the convention formed a committee to draft a bill of rights and a constitution for the state. George Mason, who was a planter, politician, and one of Virginia's delegates to the Continental Congress, drafted Virginia's Declaration of Rights. Virginia passed it **unanimously** in June 1776. A few weeks later, Thomas Jefferson used the Virginia declaration as he crafted the Declaration of Independence. In this activity, you will explore how the Virginia Declaration of Rights influenced Thomas Jefferson as he was writing the Declaration of Independence.

Read the Virginia Declaration of Rights and the Declaration of Independence. You can find the full text of the documents here. How do you think the Virginia declaration influenced Thomas Jefferson and the Declaration of Independence?

Virginia Declaration of Rights 🔍

Declaration of Independence 🔍

* Which parts are similar?

* What is different about the documents?

Create a way to present your research. Will you create a chart, a diagram, or a PowerPoint presentation? Consider the needs of your audience. What is the best way to show your information?

WORDS TO KNOW

unanimous: when a group is in full agreement.

Make Your Own Parchment

In the 1700s, important government documents were written on parchment because it is a strong and stable material. The colonists made parchment from animal skins, which were specially treated and stretched. The original Declaration of Independence was written on parchment. Other versions of the Declaration of Independence were printed on paper and read aloud throughout the colonies. In this activity, you will make a replica of the parchment used for the Declaration of Independence.

Do an Internet search to find pictures of parchment. What type of material will you use to make parchment instead of animal skins?

Old documents written on parchment usually look old and have frayed edges. How will you make your material look old and worn on the edges? What kind of liquid can you use to change the color of material? Coffee and tea are good things to use as dye. What else can you use? Experiment with different dyes and different lengths of soaking time. What works best?

EXPLORE MORE: Take your turn as an engrosser and write the preamble of the Declaration of Independence on your piece of parchment. Use your best penmanship. Do you think people were more careful back then when they printed formal documents by hand than they are now?

DID YOU KNOW?
In Europe, a high-quality parchment called vellum was made from the skins of calves, goat kids, or lambs.

ACTIVITY

Write in Calligraphy

The original Declaration of Independence is written in a beautiful calligraphy. Thomas Jefferson created the words, but have you ever wondered who actually put those words on paper? In the 1700s, official documents were usually engrossed, or copied, in a large, easy-to-read script. Master penmen or engrossers wrote in clear handwriting on important documents such as land deeds, mortgages, and more. After the Declaration of Independence was approved by the colonies, the Continental Congress ordered that it be engrossed on parchment. Many historians believe Timothy Matlack was the man who engrossed the Declaration of Independence. Matlack used a feather quill pen to handwrite the declaration.

Use lined paper or create your own lines to use as guides.

Hold your pen or marker with the tip at a 45-degree angle. Practice making basic downward strokes and curved strokes.

Now practice making different letters of the alphabet, using the guide, below. Remember to keep your pen or marker tip at a 45-degree angle.

Once you have practiced writing calligraphy letters, line a clean sheet of paper. Write a sentence or two in calligraphy. You can create your own words or copy those of the Founding Fathers. After the ink has dried, erase the pencil lines.

a b c d f g h i j k l m n o
p q r s t u v w x y z

ACTIVITY

Write the Declaration of Independence in Your Own Words

Thomas Jefferson wrote the Declaration of Independence using words and phrases common to the 1700s. Today, much of the language in the document probably sounds unfamiliar. Now it is your chance to bring the Declaration of Independence into modern times. In this activity, you will rewrite a section of the Declaration of Independence for the twenty-first century.

Read the first two paragraphs of the Declaration of Independence on page 21. What do you think the author is trying to say?

After reading the declaration, think about the following questions.

★ What do you think "unalienable rights" means?

★ According to the declaration, where do unalienable rights come from?

★ What is the purpose of government?

★ From where does government get its power?

★ Are the powers given to the government by the people limited or unlimited?

★ When should government be changed?

★ Does the fact that many of the men who signed the declaration owned slaves mean these ideas are wrong or less important? Why or why not?

DID YOU KNOW? Historians disagree about which date the Declaration of Independence was signed. Some say it was signed on July 4, 1776, and others say it was signed a month later.

Rewrite the first two paragraphs of the Declaration of Independence using your own words. Your version should include all of the major ideas from the original.

Create a Storyboard from Thomas Paine's *Common Sense*

In the years leading up to the Revolutionary War, many colonists were unhappy with the way Great Britain treated them. Even so, few people were willing to stand up against the king and Great Britain to call for change. They held out hope for a reconciliation with the king.

Published in January 1776, Thomas Paine's *Common Sense* was the first document to call for permanent separation from Great Britain. Paine's persuasive arguments convinced many Americans to accept that independence was the only way to preserve their liberty. In this activity, you will examine several quotes from *Common Sense* and create a storyboard that explains what Paine's words meant.

Read the quotes from *Common Sense* on the following page.

What was Thomas Paine trying to say in each quote? Use a dictionary to look up any words that you do not understand. How would you say the same thing in your own words?

Choose one quote. Think about how you could visually show the quote's meaning in a storyboard. This is a series of panels with drawings that show a series of scenes or events. Create scenes that show your translation of the quote or illustrate the main ideas of the quote. Display the panels of your storyboard in order.

Thomas Paine's *Common Sense*

"In the following pages I offer nothing more than simple facts, plain arguments, and common sense; and have no other preliminaries to settle with the reader, than that he will divest himself of prejudice and prepossession, and suffer his reason and his feelings to determine for themselves; that he will put on, or rather that he will not put off, the true character of a man, and generously enlarge his views beyond the present day.

"Volumes have been written on the subject of the struggle between England and America. Men of all ranks have embarked in the controversy, from different motives, and with various designs; but all have been ineffectual, and the period of debate is closed. Arms, as the last resource, decide the contest; the appeal was the choice of the King, and the Continent has accepted the challenge.

"As to government matters, it is not in the power of Britain to do this continent justice: The business of it will soon be too weighty, and intricate, to be managed with any tolerable degree of convenience, by a power, so distant from us, and so very ignorant of us; for if they cannot conquer us, they cannot govern us. . . ."

You can find the text of the entire document here. Does this essay remind you of any documents written more recently? How do you think a pamphlet with this writing would be received today?

Paine Common Sense 🔍

TRY THIS: Imagine that you are King George III. What would your reaction be to *Common Sense*? Create a new storyboard that illustrates the king's response to one of the quotes.

Chapter 2

THE CONSTITUTION OF THE UNITED STATES

A decade after the Declaration of Independence announced the creation of a new nation, the young country called the United States of America was struggling. The Americans had won their independence in the Revolutionary War, but now they had new problems.

The country had borrowed millions of dollars from other countries, from member states, and from private citizens to pay for the Revolutionary War. Now, it had to pay that debt back. But the country did not have the power to collect taxes. Instead, the Congress could only ask the states for money, and most states gave only a small portion of what Congress asked for and needed.

? ESSENTIAL QUESTION

How would your life be different if the U.S. Constitution had never been written?

In addition, trade disagreements cropped up between states. Some states refused to trade with each other. Some states taxed goods that came from other states. These policies angered the merchants and farmers who produced these goods. With so many restrictions and taxes on trade, business suffered. Unemployment rose. The nation entered an **economic depression**.

In Massachusetts, violence broke out in 1786 and 1787 when some farmers could not repay their debts and were jailed. Led by former Continental Army Captain Daniel Shays, the angry farmers attacked courts in two counties. In 1787, Shays led more than 1,000 farmers against the arsenal in Springfield, Massachusetts. Although the Massachusetts militia defeated the farmers, Shays' Rebellion caused many people to call for a stronger central government that would be able to suppress future rebellions. State leaders called for a convention to talk about revising the Articles of Confederation.

baron: a title of a member of the nobility.

supermajority: a majority that is greater than a simple majority, such as two-thirds or three-fifths.

amendment: a change or addition to a document.

WORDS TO KNOW

Constitutional Influences

When they designed the Constitution, the Founding Fathers referred to other ideas and sources. They looked at the Iroquois League, an agreement made when several Native American Iroquois nations joined together for defense. They were also influenced by ideas from Europe, such as England's Magna Carta and Parliament's representative government. Some of the Founding Fathers were influenced by the works of Enlightenment philosophers such as John Locke and **Baron** de Montesquieu.

In 1690, English philosopher John Locke wrote his ideas in *Two Treatises on Government*. He believed that all people had natural rights to life, liberty, and property. He also believed that the people had the right to rebel against the government if the government violated the people's rights.

In 1748, the French philosopher Baron de Montesquieu published *The Spirit of Laws*. He suggested that a government's power could be limited if its governing bodies were separate. Montesquieu believed that a government should be divided into three branches—legislative, executive, and judicial. Does that sound familiar?

～ THE CONSTITUTIONAL CONVENTION ～

In May 1787, 55 delegates from 12 of the 13 states arrived in Philadelphia. They came with the purpose of revising the Articles of Confederation. Only Rhode Island did not send a delegate. The state of Rhode Island did not want to be involved in creating a stronger central government. These delegates became known as the "Founding Fathers" of the United States.

In a unanimous vote, the delegates elected George Washington to lead the convention.

For four months, the 55 delegates met in private sessions. Before long, they realized that they could not revise the Articles of Confederation. The document had too many weaknesses.

- Each state had only one vote in Congress, regardless of size.

- Congress did not have the power to tax or regulate commerce.

- To pass a law, nine out of 13 colonies needed to vote for it in Congress, which was not just a simple majority but a **supermajority**.

- There was no branch of government to enforce the acts of Congress.

- There was no national court system to interpret laws and resolve disputes.

- Any **amendments** to the Articles of Confederation could be approved only by a unanimous vote.

The delegates realized that they could not fix the Articles of Confederation. Instead, they needed to write a new constitution. With this new document, the delegates wanted to create a strong central government that would unify the country.

DID YOU KNOW?

The delegates wanted the new constitution to honor the ideas and themes written in the Declaration of Independence.

THE VIRGINIA PLAN

James Madison, a delegate from Virginia, believed from the start that the country needed a new constitution. He was very active at the convention. He attended every session and took careful notes. An idea called the Virginia Plan was proposed by Madison, which called for a strong central government with three branches. A legislative branch would make laws, an executive branch would carry out laws, and a judicial branch would interpret laws and determine if they were carried out fairly and legally.

veto: to reject a decision made by a legislative body.

compromise: an agreement made with each side giving up something.

WORDS TO KNOW

Under the Virginia Plan, there would be a two-house legislature. In both houses, the number of representatives for a state would be determined by the state's population. Under this system, larger states would have more representatives, and therefore more votes, than a smaller state. This was a different system from the one outlined in the Articles of Confederation, under which each state had one vote, no matter its size.

DID YOU KNOW?

Three delegates refused to sign the Constitution: George Mason of Virginia, Edmund Randolph of Virginia, and Elbridge Gerry of Massachusetts.

The Virginia Plan also proposed a stronger central government. It called for the central government to step in and resolve disputes between the states if they could not do so themselves. Congress, and not the people, should choose the president and federal judges. The plan also proposed that the president and the federal courts could **veto** laws passed by the legislature. If there were enough votes, the two houses of the legislature could then override the veto.

∼∼∼∼∼∼ DELEGATES DEBATE ∼∼∼∼∼∼

Delegates from small and large states disagreed over the best way to send representatives to a national legislature. Delegates from the smaller states objected to Madison's Virginia Plan. If the number of representatives, and votes, was based solely on a state's population, the smaller states would have little say in the country's decisions and laws. The larger states opposed plans where each state had one vote.

Why should a state with only a few people have the same amount of power as a state with many more people?

The debate over representation went back and forth for a long time. Additionally, many delegates were uncomfortable with the strong central government that was outlined in the Virginia Plan.

Delegates from New Jersey presented the New Jersey Plan as an alternative. This plan also proposed a central government with three branches. Unlike the Virginia Plan, the New Jersey plan called for a single-house legislature. Like the Articles of Confederation, the New Jersey Plan called for each state to have one vote in the legislature, no matter its size. The New Jersey Plan also left much power with the states. The legislature would have the same powers it did under the articles, but it would also be able to tax and regulate trade among the states.

DID YOU KNOW?

Most delegates from large states favored the Virginia Plan. Delegates from smaller states preferred the New Jersey Plan.

Debates over the two plans raged for a few weeks. Several delegates, including George Washington and Benjamin Franklin, worried that a **compromise** might never be found.

bi-cameral: a legislature with two houses.

WORDS TO KNOW

~ THE GREAT COMPROMISE ~

In early July, the convention authorized a grand committee to work on a solution. The committee was made up of one delegate from each state and was chaired by Benjamin Franklin. After much debate, the committee came up with a plan for Congress.

The legislature would be **bi-cameral**, meaning that it would have two houses. Members of the upper house, called the Senate, would be chosen by the state legislatures. Each state, regardless of size, would have two members. This idea pleased the smaller states.

The lower house, called the House of Representatives, would be determined based on population. Voters in each state would directly choose their representatives. The number of representatives for each state would be based on the state's population. This idea followed the one in Madison's Virginia Plan and pleased the larger states.

On July 16, 1787, the delegates voted to approve the Great Compromise.

THE THREE-FIFTHS COMPROMISE

Now that the delegates had agreed to a plan for the country's new legislature, they turned to another issue. How should each state determine its population? This was extremely important, because the number of seats each state had in the House of Representatives was directly based on population. Population also affected the taxes each state would have to pay to the national government.

In the North, the economy relied on free men and women working in manufacturing and trade. The Southern economy relied on slaves working on plantations. The Southern states wanted to count slaves as part of their population when determining representatives. This would give them more members in the House of Representatives. However, they did not want to count slaves for tax purposes. This would allow them to pay lower taxes to the national government. The Northern states disagreed. They argued that slaves should be counted for tax purposes, but not for representation in the legislature.

DID YOU KNOW?

To get the Southern states to agree to an effective national government, the delegates at the Constitutional Convention had to compromise on the issue of slavery. They agreed Congress could not outlaw slave trade for 20 years and no state could stop an escaped slave from being returned to his or her owner.

100 slaves = 60 citizens

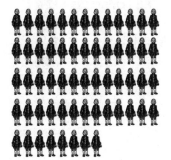

After much debate, the delegates agreed to the Three-Fifths Compromise. Under this agreement, three-fifths of the South's slave population would count toward both representation in the House of Representatives and taxes.

federalism: a division of power between the state and federal government.

WORDS TO KNOW

～ A NEW CONSTITUTION ～

After four months of debate, the delegates of the Constitutional Convention finished a new plan of government. They wrote this plan in a new document called the Constitution of the United States. On September 17, 1787, 39 delegates signed the Constitution. They hoped that this new plan would strengthen the young country and ensure its survival.

In the Constitution, the Founding Fathers set the principles of government that Americans have lived by for more than 200 years. They attempted to balance the right of people to live as they choose with a strong and effective government.

～ STATE VS. FEDERAL POWER ～

One of the biggest differences between the Articles of Confederation and the Constitution is how power is divided between the states and the federal government. Under the articles, the states had more power than the federal government.

Representative Democracy

According to the Declaration of Independence, the government gets its power from the people. This is based on the principle of popular sovereignty. In 1787, the Founding Fathers worried about giving the people too much power. They knew that people did not always choose wisely or fairly. So they created a representative democracy. In this type of government, citizens elect officials to make decisions for them. The Founding Fathers understood that, as the United States grew, a direct democracy, in which the citizens make all the decisions, would have been impossible.

Under the Constitution, the states gave up some powers to the federal government and kept other powers for themselves. This division of power between the central government and the states is called federalism.

Under the Constitution, the federal government has the power to declare war, issue money, regulate trade among the states and with other countries, and make treaties with other countries. Any powers that are not specifically granted to the federal government or denied to the states stays with the states or with the people.

For example, states have the power to regulate trade within the state. They can set up local governments. They have the authority to conduct local elections and determine who is qualified to vote in these elections. States also have the power to form public schools and provide for the safety, health, and welfare of citizens.

Some powers are shared by both the federal government and the states. For example, both have the right to tax citizens, try criminals in court, and build roads.

When the states and the federal government disagree on an issue, the Constitution is the overriding law. As a result, the federal government is generally given more power than the state governments whenever there is a conflict between the two.

DID YOU KNOW?

The Constitution includes a supremacy clause that states that the Constitution and the laws of the central government are the supreme law of the land. This means that if there is a conflict between national law and state law, national law wins.

～～～ SEPARATION OF POWERS ～～～

In the writing of the Constitution, the Founding Fathers wanted to create a strong federal government. At the same time, they were hesitant to give the federal government too much power. To limit its power, they divided the federal government into three separate branches. Under this system, different branches of the government make the laws, enforce the laws, and interpret the laws.

The legislative branch: The legislative branch of government, called the United States Congress, makes the laws of the country. This branch is bi-cameral, which means that it is divided into two houses—the Senate and the House of Representatives.

In addition to making laws, Congress also has the power to declare war, form armies, collect taxes, and set trade guidelines. The people elect members of both houses of Congress. In the House of Representatives, the number of representatives is based on a state's population. In the Senate, each state has two members. At first, each state legislature chose the senators. Since 1913, the people have elected their senators.

The executive branch: The executive branch carries out the laws of the country. This branch includes the president and vice president of the United States. The president is the commander-in-chief of the military forces. The president can also make treaties with other countries, pardon criminals, and appoint some government officials, subject to approval by the Senate.

The judicial branch: The third branch of government, the judicial branch, interprets the country's laws. This branch includes the Supreme Court, the highest court in the country. The Supreme Court and other lower federal courts hear cases about constitutional rights, disputes between the states, and laws passed by Congress. Federal judges are appointed by the president and serve for life. Under the Constitution, the Supreme Court has the final power to judge all cases brought before it. This gives the judicial branch the power to prevent other branches of government from violating the Constitution.

Three Types of Power

The Constitution gives three types of power to the federal government.

1. Delegated powers are those powers that are specifically granted to the federal government in the Constitution. Examples include the power to coin money and declare war.

2. Implied powers are not specifically stated in the Constitution, but are reasonable under the clause that gives Congress the right "to make all laws which shall be necessary and proper for carrying into execution the foregoing powers, and other power vested in the government of the United States." The Supreme Court often decides whether or not something is an implied power.

3. Inherent powers are not listed in the Constitution, but they grow out of the existence of the federal government. For example, the government has the power to add territory through exploration.

checks and balances: a system set up in the Constitution where each branch of the government has some authority over the others.

tyranny: cruel and unfair treatment by people in power.

impeach: to formally charge a public official with misconduct or a crime.

unconstitutional: not in accordance with the laws or rules of the U.S. Constitution.

WORDS TO KNOW

～ CHECKS AND BALANCES ～

The Founding Fathers included a set of **checks and balances** in the Constitution that prevents any branch of the government from becoming too powerful. Under this system of checks and balances, each branch has limiting authority over the other two branches.

For example, when Congress (legislative branch) passes a bill, it does not become a law until the president (executive branch) signs it. This gives the executive branch a way to make sure the legislative branch is not exerting too much power. If the president decides to veto a bill instead of signing it, Congress can override the veto if two-thirds of both the House of Representatives and the Senate agree.

DID YOU KNOW?

The oldest person to sign the Constitution was Benjamin Franklin (81). The youngest was Jonathan Dayton of New Jersey (26).

Limited Government

The Founding Fathers wanted to protect Americans from **tyranny**. To do this, they set up a limited government. A limited government does not have absolute authority. In the United States, the government is limited by the Constitution. This document specifically states what each branch of government can and cannot do. In addition, the Constitution specifically states that the government does not have certain powers. For example, the federal government cannot tax goods sold between states.

The legislative branch also has checks over the executive branch. For example, although the president can make treaties with other countries, the Senate must approve them. Congress also has the power to **impeach** the president, which could lead to the president being removed from office.

Both the president and Congress check the powers of the judicial branch. The president appoints federal judges and the Senate approves them. Congress can also remove federal judges from office if they break the law or behave irresponsibly.

The judicial branch can check the powers of both the executive and legislative branches. The Supreme Court interprets the meaning of laws and can strike down a law that does not follow the Constitution. It can also rule a president's actions **unconstitutional**.

RATIFICATION

The Founding Fathers drafted and approved the Constitution, but before it could become law, it had to be ratified by the states. The Founding Fathers realized that they would never get all 13 states to agree. Instead, they decided that ratification by at least nine of the 13 states would be enough to approve the Constitution.

federalist: a person who supports a strong central government.

anti-federalist: a person who supports strong state governments instead of a central government.

WORDS TO KNOW

As each state decided whether or not to ratify the Constitution, heated debates spread across the country. Some people, called **federalists**, wanted a strong central government. They supported the Constitution because it created a stronger central government. Federalists argued that the Articles of Confederation were too weak and would not protect the country. James Madison, Alexander Hamilton, and John Jay were well-known federalists.

Anti-federalists did not support a strong central government. They did not want the Constitution to replace the Articles of Confederation. Anti-federalists argued that the Constitution did not protect the basic rights and freedoms of the citizens. In addition, they argued that the Constitutional Convention was not authorized to write an entirely new document, they were only supposed to amend the articles. John Hancock, Samuel Adams, and Patrick Henry were well-known anti-federalists.

DID YOU KNOW?

Thomas Jefferson did not sign the Constitution. He was in France during the convention, where he served as the U.S. minister to France.

Each state called a special convention to ratify the Constitution. By the end of 1787, Delaware, Pennsylvania, and New Jersey had ratified the Constitution. In early 1788, three more states—Georgia, Connecticut, and Massachusetts—ratified it. A few months later, Maryland and South Carolina also ratified the Constitution. In June 1788, New Hampshire became the ninth state to ratify the Constitution. Also in June, New York and Virginia narrowly ratified the Constitution. In 1789, North Carolina voted for ratification. Rhode Island became the last state to ratify the Constitution, in 1790.

What Does It Say?

The Constitution begins with a preamble, or introduction. This section identifies the ideals that the government stands for and the document's purpose. It states:

"We the People of the United States, in Order to form a more perfect Union, establish justice, insure domestic Tranquility, provide for the common defense, promote the general Welfare, and secure the Blessings of Liberty to ourselves and our Posterity, do ordain and establish this Constitution for the United States of America."

In the main body, the Constitution mainly deals with the running of government, including the following articles.

> Article 1, which describes the powers of the legislature

> Article 2, which describes the powers of the executive branch

> Article 3, which describes the powers of the judicial branch

> Article 4, which describes the role of the states

> Article 5, which outlines the process for amending the Constitution

> Article 6, which establishes that federal law is supreme over state law when the two are in conflict

> Article 7, which sets out the requirements for ratification of the Constitution

You can read the entire Constitution here. Are there any parts you recognize? Do you think it's important for citizens to read the founding document of the U.S. government?

U.S. Constitution archives 🔍

With New Hampshire's ratification, the Constitution became the supreme law of the United States. Although it faced several crises, including the Civil War, this document has stood the test of time. The Constitution still provides a framework for the government of the United States.

? ESSENTIAL QUESTION

Now it's time to consider and discuss the Essential Question: How would your life be different if the U.S. Constitution had never been written?

47

Who Has the Power? Articles of Confederation vs. the U.S. Constitution

The delegates at the Constitutional Convention met to revise the Articles of Confederation. They ended up creating an entirely new document instead, the U.S. Constitution. While the two documents have several things in common, they also have many differences. In this activity, you will compare the two documents to find out who has the power!

The Articles of Confederation and the Constitution divide power between the states and the federal government in different ways. Look at the Articles of Confederation and the text of the Constitution here.

Articles of Confederation 🔍

U.S. Constitution 🔍

How is each of the following treated in the two documents? Who has the power under each document? Think of a way to organize your research.

* Legislature
* Members of Congress
* Voting in Congress
* Appointment of members of Congress
* Term of legislative office
* Term limits for legislative office
* Congressional pay
* Executive office

* National judiciary or courts
* How disputes between states are resolved
* New states
* Amendments
* Military—Army, Navy
* Power to coin money
* Taxes
* Ratification

EXPLORE MORE: Create a game using the differences between the Articles of Confederation and the Constitution. Design a game board or playing cards and write up a set of rules. Or, can you develop and code a new video game?

Debate at the Constitutional Convention

At the Constitutional Convention, the delegates debated the Constitution and how the country should divide government powers between the states and a central government. Some delegates supported a strong central government and urged others to support the Constitution. Other delegates wanted power to remain with the states and argued that the Constitution did little to protect the basic rights of citizens. In this activity, you will take the role of one of these delegates and argue his position.

Write the names of the following delegates on separate notecards.

* George Mason (anti-federalist)
* Richard Henry Lee (anti-federalist)
* Elbridge Gerry (anti-federalist)
* Alexander Hamilton (federalist)
* John Jay (federalist)
* James Madison (federalist)

Select one person to be the moderator of the debate. Each remaining person will select a notecard to choose their role in the debate. Use the Internet to learn a little more about these founders here.

America's founders online 🔍

Taking on the roles of the different founders, debate the following topics.

* the Articles of Confederation
* the Constitution
* the need for a bill of rights to protect the basic rights of the people

How would you solve the differences between the federalists and the anti-federalists? Can your "delegates" negotiate a compromise that each side can support?

CONSTITUTIONAL CONVENTION

Checks and Balances

The Constitution includes checks and balances on each of the three branches of government to ensure that no one branch becomes too powerful. Let's see how this works in practice.

Divide participants into three groups. Each group represents one of the three branches of government. Choose a goal for each group to achieve. For example, the executive branch might want to replace the "Pledge of Allegiance" in schools with a song or the legislative branch may want to make a law requiring ice cream in all school lunches.

checks and balances chart 🔎

Have each group brainstorm a list of actions and steps that their branch has the power to take in order to accomplish their goal.

Bring the three groups together and have each share their goal and the actions that they plan to take to accomplish it. What type of presentation will you create?

After everyone has listened to each group's presentation, have the groups separate again to brainstorm how they would use checks and balances to prevent the other two branches of government from accomplishing their goals. What three specific actions can they take?

Bring the groups together again. How can each group prevent the other branches from accomplishing their goals? How does the system of checks and balances work to limit the power of any single branch?

EXPLORE MORE: Take one goal and brainstorm a way to compromise and get it passed. How can the different branches of government work together?

ACTIVITY

The Preamble's Promises

In the Preamble to the Constitution, the Founding Fathers made several promises about the purpose of government. In this activity, we will investigate exactly what they meant by this statement and how they put these promises into practice.

"We the people of the United States, in order to form a more perfect union, establish justice, insure domestic tranquility, provide for the common defense, promote the general welfare, and secure the blessings of liberty to ourselves and our posterity, do ordain and establish this Constitution for the United States of America."

What promises are made to the people in the Preamble? List each one on a separate piece of paper in your history journal.

Although the wording of the Preamble might sound formal or stiff, its purpose is still the same today as it was when it was written in 1787. What do you think each promise means? Rewrite each promise in your own words.

How did the Founding Fathers put these promises into practice? What did they include in the Constitution that addresses each promise? Take another look at the Constitution.

U.S. Constitution 🔍

For each promise, write an example of how the idea is in action in the United States today. Which promises are the most important? Explain why you choose them.

EXPLORE MORE: Using several newspapers or magazines, find headlines, photographs, and articles that illustrate the promises in the Preamble in action today. Explain how these examples illustrate the beliefs of the writers of the Constitution.

ACTIVITY

51

Chapter 3

THE BILL OF RIGHTS

AMENDING THE CONSTITUTION

Americans treasure their personal rights, such as the freedom of speech, freedom of the press, and the right to a fair and speedy trial. Did you know that these iconic rights were not originally part of the Constitution? Instead, these rights were added to the Constitution as amendments.

The Founding Fathers knew that the Constitution was not perfect. It would need to be altered as circumstances changed for the young country. The Founding Fathers created a method for making important changes to the document in years to come. A change to the Constitution is called an amendment. So far, the Constitution has been amended 27 times.

? ESSENTIAL QUESTION

Why is it important to be able to change the Constitution?

～～～～～ THE BILL OF RIGHTS ～～～～～

When the states were debating whether or not to ratify the Constitution, many people were upset that the Constitution did not include a bill of rights. They believed a bill of rights was necessary to protect the hard-won personal freedoms of Americans.

DID YOU KNOW?

In drafting the Bill of Rights, James Madison drew heavily on the ideas in the Virginia Declaration of Rights, written by George Mason. The Virginia Declaration had also influenced Thomas Jefferson's writing of the Declaration of Independence.

Federalists believed that the Constitution did not need a bill of rights, because the people and states held all powers not specifically given to the federal government. In addition, they argued that most states already had a bill of rights. Anti-federalists argued that a national bill of rights was essential to protect individual rights.

The first federal Congress took on the issue of a bill of rights. Virginian James Madison, a member of the House of Representatives, was opposed to adding a bill of rights at first. He changed his mind when it became clear that promising to add a bill of rights would help to get the Constitution ratified.

Many members of the House believed that Congress did not have the authority to change the Constitution's wording. Instead, Madison presented the proposed changes as a list of amendments. Of these, the House approved 17 amendments. Of those 17, the Senate approved 12 amendments in 1789. By December 15, 1791, 10 of the 12 amendments had been ratified by the states.

These 10 amendments became known collectively as the Bill of Rights.

due process: the legal requirement that the government must respect all legal rights that are owed to a person.

WORDS TO KNOW

∽ WHAT DOES IT SAY? ∽

The Bill of Rights describes the rights of all people in America. It places strict limits on the power of the national government to infringe on individual rights. For example, the founders believed that each person has the right to practice their own religion. Placing this protection in the First Amendment prevents Congress from making a law that limits this right.

The First Amendment is one of the most well-known amendments to the Constitution. It protects five basic American freedoms—freedom of religion, freedom of speech, freedom of the press, freedom of assembly, and freedom to petition the government. The First Amendment gives you the right to worship freely and to speak your mind freely. It allows journalists to report all parts of the news, without being controlled by the government. It also allows you to gather to support a political candidate or to protest a government policy.

The Second Amendment guarantees Americans the right to bear arms and to serve in a state militia. Americans were nervous about being forced to house soldiers as they had been under British rule. Because of this, the Third Amendment limits the government's power to make Americans house soldiers.

The Fourth Amendment protects people against unreasonable searches and seizures. Under the Fifth Amendment, people accused of a crime have specific rights. No person can be put on trial for a serious crime without being indicted or formally accused by a grand jury. The Fifth Amendment also protects people from being tried more than once for the same crime. It guarantees that a person accused of a crime cannot be forced to testify against themselves. The Fifth Amendment guarantees that **due process** of law will be followed, meaning that the trial will follow procedures put in place by law and the Constitution. The Fifth Amendment also protects property rights.

The government's power to take private property for public use, called the power of eminent domain, is limited under this amendment.

DID YOU KNOW? Since 1787, more than 9,000 amendments have been proposed. Only 27 have been approved.

The Sixth, Seventh, and Eighth Amendments guarantee additional rights to people accused of crimes in criminal or civil trials. The Ninth and Tenth Amendments specifically state that rights listed in the Constitution are not the only rights of the American people. Any powers that the Constitution does not specifically grant to the national government remain with the states or the people.

THE PROCESS FOR AMENDING THE CONSTITUTION

The Founding Fathers did not want future leaders to be able to change the Constitution too easily. Therefore, they created an amendment process that is very involved. There are two main steps in the amendment process—proposal and ratification.

WORDS TO KNOW

Prohibition: the period of time from 1920 to 1933 when the sale of alcoholic beverages was banned—or prohibited—in the United States.

proclamation: a public or official announcement.

First, an amendment must be proposed. It can be proposed in two ways. In one way, two-thirds of the members of both houses of Congress must vote for a proposed amendment. In the second way, two-thirds of the state legislatures must request a national convention, where an amendment is proposed. So far, this type of national convention has never been called.

Once an amendment has been proposed, it must be ratified by three-fourths of the states. There are two ways a state can ratify an amendment. First, the state can hold a vote in the state legislature. The other way to ratify an amendment is by calling a special state convention.

DID YOU KNOW? The Twenty-first Amendment, which brought about an end to **Prohibition** in 1933, is the only amendment that has been ratified by state conventions.

Congress can set a time limit on ratification. Since the early 1900s, Congress has given the states a seven-year time limit to ratify an amendment. If the states do not ratify the amendment within the time limit, the amendment dies. When needed, Congress has the option to extend the time limit for ratification.

Sometimes, it takes a very long time to get an amendment ratified. For example, the Twenty-seventh Amendment was first proposed in 1789 as one of the original 12 amendments. But Congress did not set a time limit on it. Therefore, it did not die, and eventually it was ratified and became an amendment in 1992, when Michigan became the 38th state to ratify it! The Twenty-seventh Amendment prevents Congress from passing immediate pay raises for itself.

THE RECONSTRUCTION AMENDMENTS: THE THIRTEENTH, FOURTEENTH, AND FIFTEENTH AMENDMENTS

Since the Constitution was ratified, several amendments have made notable changes to it. The Thirteenth, Fourteenth, and Fifteenth Amendments, known as the Reconstruction Amendments, were ratified in the years directly following the Civil War. This group of amendments dealt with rights for former slaves. Remember, the Constitution did not make any attempt to abolish slavery when it was first written.

In 1863, President Abraham Lincoln issued the Emancipation **Proclamation**, declaring that all people held as slaves in the South were free. Lincoln feared that the Emancipation Proclamation would be overturned when the war ended. He wanted a constitutional amendment that would guarantee that slavery would no longer exist anywhere in the United States.

In January 1865, Congress formally proposed the Thirteenth Amendment, which abolished slavery. It also prohibited a person from being bound into personal service because of debt. It was ratified by three-fourths of the states by December 6, 1865.

Ratified in 1868, the Fourteenth Amendment established that all people are entitled to equal protection of the law. It granted American citizenship, civil liberties, due process, and equal protection to former slaves and their descendants. It defined citizenship as a right given to all people born in the United States.

Confederate: the government established by the Southern slave-owning states of the United States after they left the Union in 1860 and 1861. Called the Confederate States of America or the Confederacy.

civil right: a right that allows a person to participate fully in civil and political life without discrimination.

discrimination: to deny a group of people opportunities based on things such as race or gender.

suffrage: the right to vote.

WORDS TO KNOW

The Fourteenth Amendment put penalties in place if a state denied citizens the right to vote. It barred former **Confederate** leaders from holding state or federal office and also denied federal funding for the Confederacy's war debts. Former slaveholders were banned from collecting money to compensate for the loss of their slaves.

Most of the Southern states rejected the Fourteenth Amendment, but it was ratified by the required three-fourths of states in July 1868. In the years since its ratification, the equal protection clause of the Fourteenth Amendment has been used by many people to fight for equal rights.

In the 1950s, the Supreme Court used the due process part of the Fourteenth Amendment to protect **civil rights** and civil liberties.

The Fifteenth Amendment of 1870 prohibited states from denying voting rights to citizens based on their race, color, or if they were former slaves. Despite this amendment, many Southern states still denied African Americans the right to vote by using poll taxes, literacy tests, whites-only primaries, intimidation, and even the threat of violence. To enforce the Fifteenth Amendment, Congress passed stricter laws in the 1950s and 1960s to end racial **discrimination** for voting rights.

THE NINETEENTH AMENDMENT: WOMEN'S SUFFRAGE

When the Constitution was ratified in 1789, it did not grant liberty to all people. In the first presidential election in 1789, only white, male property owners were eligible to vote. Since then, the rights and liberties granted in the Constitution have been expanded to include more people through laws, Supreme Court decisions, and constitutional amendments.

The Fifteenth Amendment extended the right to vote to former male slaves. A law passed by Congress in 1924 extended the right to vote to American Indians. With the Nineteenth Amendment, women gained the right to vote. Ratified in 1920, the Nineteenth Amendment prohibited states from denying voting rights based on gender. The ratification of this amendment was a landmark victory for the women's **suffrage** movement, which had battled to gain equal rights for years.

DID YOU KNOW?

Ratified in 1913, the Sixteenth Amendment authorized a federal income tax on all citizens.

The Bill of Rights

Amendment I

Congress shall make no law respecting an establishment of religion, or prohibiting the free exercise thereof; or abridging the freedom of speech, or of the press; or the right of the people peaceably to assemble, and to petition the government for a redress of grievances.

Amendment II

A well regulated militia, being necessary to the security of a free state, the right of the people to keep and bear arms, shall not be infringed.

Amendment III

No soldier shall, in time of peace be quartered in any house, without the consent of the owner, nor in time of war, but in a manner to be prescribed by law.

Amendment IV

The right of the people to be secure in their persons, houses, papers, and effects, against unreasonable searches and seizures, shall not be violated, and no warrants shall issue, but upon probable cause, supported by oath or affirmation, and particularly describing the place to be searched, and the persons or things to be seized.

Amendment V

No person shall be held to answer for a capital, or otherwise infamous crime, unless on a presentment or indictment of a grand jury, except in cases arising in the land or naval forces, or in the militia, when in actual service in time of war or public danger; nor shall any person be subject for the same offense to be twice put in jeopardy of life or limb; nor shall be compelled in any criminal case to be a witness against himself, nor be deprived of life, liberty, or property, without due process of law; nor shall private property be taken for public use, without just compensation.

Amendment VI

In all criminal prosecutions, the accused shall enjoy the right to a speedy and public trial, by an impartial jury of the state and district wherein the crime shall have been committed, which district shall have been previously ascertained by law, and to be informed of the nature and cause of the accusation; to be confronted with the witnesses against him; to have compulsory process for obtaining witnesses in his favor, and to have the assistance of counsel for his defense.

Amendment VII

In suits at common law, where the value in controversy shall exceed twenty dollars, the right of trial by jury shall be preserved, and no fact tried by a jury, shall be otherwise reexamined in any court of the United States, than according to the rules of the common law.

Amendment VIII

Excessive bail shall not be required, nor excessive fines imposed, nor cruel and unusual punishments inflicted.

Amendment IX

The enumeration in the Constitution, of certain rights, shall not be construed to deny or disparage others retained by the people.

Amendment X

The powers not delegated to the United States by the Constitution, nor prohibited by it to the states, are reserved to the states respectively, or to the people.

ESSENTIAL QUESTION

Now it's time to consider and discuss the Essential Question: Why is it important to be able to change the Constitution?

Propose a Constitutional Amendment

Since the Constitution became effective in 1789, there have been only 27 amendments that have been successfully ratified. All members of Congress have the chance to make a change to the Constitution and propose an amendment. What would you want to change?

Review the 27 amendments to the Constitution. Amendments 1–10 (the Bill of Rights) can be found on pages 60 and 61. Amendments 11–27 can be found online.

Constitution: Amendments 11-27 🔍

Imagine that you are a member of Congress who has been appointed to a committee to create a new amendment. Brainstorm ideas for your amendment.

* What do you want to change?

* How can you make life better for people?

* Where do you see injustices?

* Choose the idea that you feel has the most promise.

Create a proposal for your amendment. Will you use paper, PowerPoint software, or something else? Be creative! Include an explanation of why your amendment is needed and how it will benefit the country. Present your proposed amendment.

EXPLORE MORE: Instead of supporting the proposed amendment, what if you opposed it? Write a short essay that argues against the amendment. How do you balance the rights of an individual with the needs of the entire population?

Is a College Education a Constitutional Right?

The cost of college is higher than ever. Students who cannot afford to pay are often unable to go to college. This has caused many people to think about whether a college education is a right that should be guaranteed for all Americans. Having a college degree gives a person many advantages in life. Should the Constitution be amended to guarantee a college education for all Americans?

Consider whether or not you believe a free college education is a right. What do you think? Why?

Should the right to a free college education be added as an amendment to the Constitution? Why or why not?

Imagine that you are a member of Congress and an amendment that would guarantee a college education to all citizens is proposed. Prepare a presentation to support or oppose this amendment. What points do you make to support your argument?

EXPLORE MORE: Think about another issue, such as health care. Is free health care a basic right? Should there be an amendment guaranteeing free health care for all citizens? Why or why not? Have you heard debates about college tuition and health care on the news? What do other people think about these issues?

Changing Times: Debate Over the Second Amendment

In 1791, the Founding Fathers and the country voted to include the Second Amendment in the Bill of Rights. Society has changed in many ways since the Founding Fathers wrote the Second Amendment. The debate over the right to own guns is very controversial. People on both sides feel very strongly about it. In this activity, you will think about both sides of this debate and rewrite the Second Amendment for today's changing times.

The Second Amendment states: *"A well regulated Militia, being necessary to the security of a free State, the right of the people to keep and bear Arms, shall not be infringed."* Think about the differences between 1776 and today.

* Why were guns necessary in 1776?

* Why are guns necessary today?

* Do you believe that people in America need guns?

* What are the differences in society and culture between 1776 and today? Consider topics such as crime levels, the number of accidental gun deaths, and the physical power of guns.

Consider the guns of 1776 and the ways that the guns available today are similar and different.

* Does the type of gun matter? Why or why not?

* Is it important that there are no limits placed on the kinds of guns people can have?

* Do you think the government should have the right to tell you what type of gun you can have?

Some people argue that if everyone carried a gun, then criminals would be less likely to commit crimes. Do you agree with this argument? Why or why not?

Some people believe that the government should pass stricter laws about who can own guns. Other people believe that this infringes on Second Amendment rights. What do you think?

* Should the government be able to make people wait 30 days to get a gun?

* Should the government be able to do a background check on anyone who wants to buy a gun?

* Do you agree or disagree with these ideas?

* What problems can occur when people have guns in their homes?

* Is there any way to prevent accidental gun shootings?

Some people believe they should be allowed to carry their guns with them anywhere, anytime, because they have the right to protect themselves. Others feel there should be limits placed on where people can carry a concealed weapon. What do you think?

Read the newspaper, listen to the news on the radio, or watch it on TV. What can you learn about the Second Amendment from these sources? Does what you hear or read influence your views? Rewrite the Second Amendment so that it says what you believe the country should do about guns. Or propose a new amendment to reflect your views about guns.

EXPLORE MORE: Would you change any other amendments in the Bill of Rights? Explain why or not and how you might make those changes to one or more of the first 10 amendments.

The First Amendment and You

The First Amendment is one of the best known in the Bill of Rights. In this activity, you will see how the First Amendment protects your rights.

The First Amendment states: *"Congress shall make no law respecting an establishment of religion, or prohibiting the free exercise thereof; or abridging the freedom of speech, or of the press; or the right of the people peaceably to assemble, and to petition the government for a redress of grievances."*

Think about the five rights protected by the First Amendment. What are they? How can you exercise each of these rights? Organize your ideas to show each right and list examples of how each applies to your life.

Sometimes, First Amendment rights are violated. Consider the following scenarios. Which right is involved? Do you think the First Amendment was violated? Why or why not?

* Your parents insist you attend church every Sunday.

* Your public school begins an assembly with a student-led prayer.

* Your public school principal says you cannot come to school as long as your hair is dyed green.

* You are suspended from public school for refusing to say the "Pledge of Allegiance."

* Your public school principal objects to the content in the school newspaper and **censors** it.

* The police arrest a reporter for writing an anti-government article.

* Your public school principal gives you detention for attending a protest demonstration during the school day.

EXPLORE MORE: Did you know that the First Amendment does not apply to parents? Why is this a good idea? Or is it not a good idea? Take one side of the position and argue it, giving examples and details to support your position.

ACTIVITY

66

WORDS TO KNOW

censor: to examine books, movies, letters, etc., in order to remove things that are considered to be offensive or harmful to society.

Chapter 4

OTHER IMPORTANT DOCUMENTS

Everyone knows about the Declaration of Independence, the Constitution, and the Bill of Rights. But what about the Federalist Papers and the Declaration of Sentiments? These documents, along with others, have played an important role in shaping our country's history. By exploring these documents, we can learn how they have added to the American tradition of democracy.

In 1787, the delegates at the Constitutional Convention drafted the Constitution and sent it out to the states for approval. But ratification was not a slam dunk. The public was divided over the Constitution. Some people supported it, while many others were unwilling to give the federal government more power. In several states, debate over the Constitution ignited.

? ESSENTIAL QUESTION

What are some of the qualities of a document that makes a difference in history?

In the fall of 1787, the debate over ratification of the Constitution was going strong in New York. Newspapers and magazines ran essays against the Constitution. Most of these essays argued that a powerful central government would threaten the rights of the people. Anti-federalists feared the states would lose too much power under the Constitution. And with weakened states, the country would be vulnerable to a power-hungry federal government.

The anti-federalists asked why they should ratify a Constitution that would create the same problems that caused the Revolutionary War.

～ THE FEDERALIST PAPERS (1787-1788) ～

In October 1787, three supporters and writers of the Constitution—Alexander Hamilton, James Madison, and John Jay—joined to argue for ratifying the Constitution. They secretly published a series of essays under the pen name "Publius" in New York magazines. In these essays, Publius argued that the Constitution was needed to preserve the country. He explained that the Articles of Confederation created a government that was too weak to be effective. Publius argued that giving the federal government more power would help all Americans.

For about a year, Hamilton, Madison, and Jay took turns writing the essays, 85 in all. These essays became known as the Federalist Papers. The essays had two purposes—to explain the Constitution and to persuade the public to ratify it.

DID YOU KNOW? Alexander Hamilton later served in the Presidential Cabinet as the first secretary of the treasury. You can see his picture on the front of a $10 bill.

Introduction to the Federalist Papers

Alexander Hamilton wrote the introduction to the Federalist Papers, first published in the *Independent Journal* in 1787.

"AFTER an unequivocal experience of the inefficiency of the subsisting federal government, you are called upon to deliberate on a new Constitution for the United States of America. The subject speaks its own importance; comprehending in its consequences nothing less than the existence of the UNION, the safety and welfare of the parts of which it is composed, the fate of an empire in many respects the most interesting in the world."

You can read the rest of the Federalist Papers here. What makes these essays persuasive?

Federalist Papers 🔎

In the first essays, they wrote about the need for a new Constitution. The country was failing. The states were acting in their own best interests, not for the good of the whole country. Instead of working together, the states competed against each other. Without a strong central government, the writers argued, the country would crumble.

After explaining the problem, the writers then explained the reasons the Constitution was good. They argued that a strong central government would be good for the people. It would bring **prosperity** to the country. It would be able to create a stronger military to better defend the citizens. It would also be able to build better relationships with other countries.

Publius explained how the three branches of government would work. The three men reassured the public that the Constitution had enough checks and balances to prevent any person, state, or branch of government from becoming too powerful. They also explained why each part of the Constitution was important.

equality: having equal rights, opportunities, and status.

activist: someone who works for social or political change.

sentiment: a view, feeling, or complaint.

WORDS TO KNOW

Between October 1787 and May 1788, the essays appeared frequently in the press, sometimes as often as three or four per week. Because they were published so quickly, it was difficult for the people who opposed the Constitution to respond to all of the arguments the men presented.

The Federalist Papers became so popular that they were published together in two books in the spring of 1788. The books were successful and the public was persuaded to support ratification. In July 1788, New York became the 11th state to ratify the Constitution. Some people believe that the Federalist Papers played an important part in convincing New York to ratify the Constitution. After the Federalist Papers were published, other states that had been struggling to ratify the Constitution also began to support ratification.

DID YOU KNOW?

John Jay served as the first chief justice of the Supreme Court.

The Federalist Papers give Americans an important look at what the writers of the Constitution were thinking. Madison and Hamilton had helped write the Constitution. Their essays in the Federalist Papers help us understand their thoughts and beliefs.

The Federalist Papers served as one of the main arguments for the Constitution.

～ THE DECLARATION OF SENTIMENTS (1848) ～

In the Declaration of Independence, Thomas Jefferson wrote, "All men are created equal, that they are endowed by their Creator with certain unalienable Rights, that among these are Life, Liberty and the pursuit of Happiness." Yet in the early years of the United States, **equality** only applied to white males of a certain status. Women could not vote. In some states, they could not own property.

In the mid-1800s, many women began to stand up for change. They called for equal rights and greater freedoms. In particular, they called for the right to vote.

In 1848, a group of women organized a convention in Seneca Falls, New York. Several hundred women and men interested in the women's rights movement attended the convention, including **activists** Lucretia Mott and Elizabeth Cady Stanton. The convention's goal was to discuss women's rights and how to gain these rights. At the conclusion of the convention, the delegates agreed that they should focus on suffrage, or the right to vote, for women.

The delegates also approved the Declaration of **Sentiments**. Written primarily by Stanton, this document was a statement of the goals of the women's movement. Stanton modeled it after the Declaration of Independence, but specifically included women in her version.

WORDS TO KNOW

abolitionist: someone who believed that slavery should be abolished, or ended.

secede: to withdraw from a political alliance.

The Declaration of Sentiments began with a preamble that stated several universal truths, one of which is that "all men and women are created equal."

After the introduction, the declaration listed the various ways in which men and women were not treated equally and the ways men treated women as inferior people. These complaints included the inability to vote, the lack of property rights, and the lack of legal status once married.

In its conclusion, the declaration demanded that all of the listed inequalities be immediately fixed by federal, state, and local governments. It promised that the signers would work ceaselessly until women achieved equal rights. At the end of conference, 100 delegates signed the Declaration of Sentiments. Signers included Stanton and Mott, along with **abolitionist** Frederick Douglass.

Upon its publication, the Declaration of Sentiments received mixed reviews from people at the Seneca Falls Convention and across the country. Some people praised it, while others criticized it. Many of the delegates worried that the demand for women's suffrage, the right to vote, was too much to ask for and too difficult to achieve. Instead, they suggested that pushing for equality in general might be a more realistic goal. A group of 100 men and women passed 12 resolutions that included women's right to vote, equality for all people regardless of race or ethnicity, and opposition to any law that oppressed women.

DID YOU KNOW?

Opponents of the Declaration of Sentiments used it to mock the women's movement. They called the women unfeminine and immoral. In spite of the ridicule, Stanton, Mott, and other leaders continued to fight for women's rights.

What Happened to the Declaration of Sentiments?

The original Declaration of Sentiments is missing. There is no record of it after Frederick Douglass took it with him to publish in his newspaper after the conference. In 2015, a White House staff member began a community awareness campaign to locate the missing document, using the hashtag #FindTheSentiments.

The struggle for equal rights would stretch on for decades. More than 70 years later, in 1920, the Nineteenth Amendment to the Constitution finally gave women the right to vote. Even after this milestone, women continue to struggle for equal treatment in the workplace and in other areas of society. Today, the Declaration of Sentiments remains one of the most important documents in the U.S. women's rights movement.

∼∼ EMANCIPATION PROCLAMATION (1863) ∼∼

In 1862, the United States was in the middle of the bitter Civil War. The issue of slavery had created tension between the Northern and Southern states for decades. Many of the Southern states had **seceded** from the Union because they believed President Abraham Lincoln and the federal government would interfere in their rights and their practice of slavery.

At first, Lincoln and the North entered the Civil War to reunite the country, not to end slavery. Two years into the war, with no end in sight, Lincoln realized that he needed to expand the goals of the war. He also needed to gain support for the North from antislavery groups. He decided that ending slavery would accomplish both goals.

ultimatum: a final demand.

WORDS TO KNOW

Lincoln discussed his idea with his advisors. Roger Taney, the chief justice of the Supreme Court, told Lincoln that he did not have the right under the Constitution to end slavery. Lincoln disagreed. He believed that the Constitution gave him, as the country's leader, the power to defend and preserve the Union. He argued that ending slavery and setting the South's slaves free would help do this.

Lincoln prepared an official public announcement. He waited until a major victory for the Union armies to make the announcement. In September 1862, Union armies claimed victory at the Battle of Antietam. Lincoln decided the time was right for his proclamation.

On September 22, 1862, he issued his public announcement, which would be known as the Emancipation Proclamation. In the proclamation, Lincoln issued an **ultimatum** to the Confederate states. If they did not stop their rebellion, he would free their slaves. Not one Southern state agreed to stop fighting, and the Emancipation Proclamation went into effect on January 1, 1863.

The Emancipation Proclamation set free millions of slaves in the Confederate states.

Emancipation Proclamation

"And by virtue of the power, and for the purpose aforesaid, I do order and declare that all persons held as slaves within said designated States, and parts of States, are, and henceforward shall be free; and that the Executive government of the United States, including the military and naval authorities thereof, will recognize and maintain the freedom of said persons."

You can read the entire Emancipation Proclamation here. How is the language different from the language you find in speeches today?

Emancipation Proclamation archives 🔎

Some Americans opposed the Emancipation Proclamation. They claimed that the Emancipation Proclamation did not actually free any slaves. It did not apply to slaves in loyal border states or slaves in areas under Union control, such as New Orleans. It only applied to areas outside Union control. Others argued that the president did not have the power under the Constitution to free the slaves.

Lincoln's Emancipation Proclamation gave the war new meaning for many people in the North. The war had become a fight against slavery. The proclamation also discouraged countries that had already abolished slavery, such as England and France, from supporting the South. As Union armies entered more land, more slaves were freed. Lincoln was proved right—the Emancipation Proclamation changed the course of the Civil War.

DID YOU KNOW?

The Emancipation Proclamation did not abolish slavery in the United States. That would happen after the Civil War with the Thirteenth Amendment to the Constitution in 1865.

GETTYSBURG ADDRESS (1863)

One of the most important historical documents in American history was actually a speech given by President Abraham Lincoln. In the summer of 1863, Union and Confederate forces met in one of the bloodiest battles of the Civil War. From July 1 to 3, 1863, they fought near Gettysburg, a small town in Pennsylvania. Combined, the two armies suffered nearly 51,000 **casualties** during this three-day battle. Weakened by their losses and unable to push farther into Northern land, the Confederate forces retreated and the Union claimed victory.

The Battle of Gettysburg became a turning point in the Civil War. Confederate forces would never again be strong enough to threaten the Union.

In November 1863, Lincoln attended a dedication ceremony at a cemetery built to honor the war's dead. He sat and listened while Edward Everett, a famous speaker, gave a two-hour dedication speech. Then Lincoln himself stood and spoke. His speech was not nearly as long as Everett's—it lasted only about two minutes. His words, however, are recognized as one of the finest speeches ever made.

In his speech, which would become known as the Gettysburg Address, Lincoln reminded Americans why the Union soldiers had died. He spoke about the Founding Fathers and drew from the Declaration of Independence.

Lincoln talked about the principles of liberty and equality, that the country was based on the idea that "all men are created equal." This idea was controversial at the time, because the Constitution did not explicitly say anything about equality. The idea of equality came from the Declaration of Independence. Yet Lincoln's speech showed that he believed the Declaration of Independence stated what the Founding Fathers wanted for America and its people.

Lincoln's Gettysburg Address

"Fourscore and seven years ago our fathers brought forth on this continent a new nation, conceived in liberty and dedicated to the proposition that all men are created equal. Now we are engaged in a great civil war, testing whether that nation or any nation so conceived and so dedicated can long endure. We are met on a great battlefield of that war. We have come to dedicate a portion of that field as a final resting-place for those who here gave their lives that that nation might live. It is altogether fitting and proper that we should do this. But in a larger sense, we cannot dedicate, we cannot consecrate, we cannot hallow this ground. The brave men, living and dead who struggled here have consecrated it far above our poor power to add or detract. The world will little note nor long remember what we say here, but it can never forget what they did here. It is for us the living rather to be dedicated here to the unfinished work which they who fought here have thus far so nobly advanced. It is rather for us to be here dedicated to the great task remaining before us—that from these honored dead we take increased devotion to that cause for which they gave the last full measure of devotion—that we here highly resolve that these dead shall not have died in vain, that this nation under God shall have a new birth of freedom, and that government of the people, by the people, for the people shall not perish from the earth."

—Abraham Lincoln

Lincoln also spoke about the ongoing civil war, reminding Americans that the men who had died in battle had given their lives to help preserve the Union. He urged those still living to carry on the fight so that the dead soldiers would not have died in vain. He urged Americans to keep the country together so that democracy could survive.

When the Civil War began, Lincoln's main goal was to preserve the United States. He believed that bringing the Southern states back into the Union was the best way to achieve this goal. Over time, Lincoln acknowledged that the war's goals had changed to include ending slavery. Today, the Gettysburg Address is viewed as one of the most important speeches in American history.

DID YOU KNOW? Abraham Lincoln thought the Gettysburg Address was a failure because it did not get much reaction from the crowd.

CIVIL RIGHTS ACT (1964)

After the Civil War, Congress passed several amendments to the U.S. Constitution. The Thirteenth Amendment abolished slavery. The Fourteenth and Fifteenth Amendments set out rights for all people and gave rights to the newly freed slaves. The Fourteenth Amendment made every person born in the United States a citizen, while the Fifteenth Amendment gave African American men the right to vote.

Many white Southerners were angry that they were forced to end slavery. They helped pass state laws that made it hard for African Americans to be treated equally. These laws, called Jim Crow laws, **segregated** people based on race. Jim Crow laws forced African Americans to use separate waiting rooms, separate bathrooms, and separate public transportation and to go to separate schools.

**Nearly a century after the end of slavery,
discrimination based on race was still
widespread in the United States.**

Fed up with discrimination, more and more people called for change. They wanted civil rights for all citizens, regardless of race. They believed that federal legislation was needed to ensure equal rights for all people.

In 1963, President John F. Kennedy urged the country to take action to guarantee civil rights for all Americans. Later, he proposed that Congress pass civil rights legislation that would address voting rights, public accommodations, school desegregation, and other discrimination issues. After Kennedy was assassinated in November 1963, Lyndon Johnson became president. As a senator, Johnson had worked for civil rights. In his new role as president, Johnson worked with civil rights leaders, including Dr. Martin Luther King Jr., to create the Civil Rights Act.

Kennedy's Civil Rights Address

President Kennedy cited some interesting statistics in his 1963 speech on civil rights, including the following.

"The Negro baby born in America today, regardless of the section of the Nation in which he is born, has about one-half as much chance of completing a high school as a white baby born in the same place on the same day, one-third as much chance of completing college, one-third as much chance of becoming a professional man, twice as much chance of becoming unemployed, about one-seventh as much chance of earning $10,000 a year, a life expectancy which is 7 years shorter, and the prospects of earning only half as much."

How do you think this differs from today's statistics? Do more African Americans attend college and work in higher-paying jobs now? Do some research and compare the statistics of today to those of the 1960s.

John Kennedy civil rights address 🔍

Passing the Civil Rights Act through Congress was not an easy task. Opponents such as Senator Barry Goldwater from Arizona claimed that it violated states' rights. But in 1964, supporters finally gained enough votes in both the House and Senate to pass the act. On July 2, 1964, President Johnson signed the Civil Rights Act of 1964 into law.

The Civil Rights Act guaranteed equal rights to all people, no matter their race, color, religion, gender, or national origin. The act outlawed segregation in businesses, such as theaters and restaurants. It banned discrimination in hiring. It also ended segregation in public places, such as libraries and public schools. Although it did not end racism in America, the Civil Rights Act of 1964 is viewed as one of the most important pieces of legislation in American history.

ESSENTIAL QUESTION

Now it's time to consider and discuss the Essential Question: What are some of the qualities of a document that makes a difference in history?

Write Your Own
Declaration of Independence

In 1776, the American colonists fought for their independence from Great Britain. Now it is your turn to write your own personal Declaration of Independence.

Think about what type of independence you would like to have. Do you want independence from school and homework, rules at home, the tyranny of an older sibling, or something else? Be creative!

Write a draft of your own Declaration of Independence. Use the real Declaration of Independence as a model. Make sure that you include the following.

* **A preamble:** Discuss the reasons why you are writing the declaration.

* **Declaration of rights:** Explain what you believe and the ideals behind your document.

* **List of complaints:** Name the person/persons to whom you are making your complaints. List the specific complaints that you have with them.

* **Statement of prior attempts to solve the problem:** List how you have already tried to solve the problem and your complaints.

* **Declaration of Independence:** Describe how you want things to change because of your declaration. What would be different if you were independent?

DID YOU KNOW?

The Civil Rights Act of 1964 was later expanded to include disabled Americans, the elderly, and women in college athletics.

Share your Declaration of Independence with the group you are declaring your independence from.

* What is their reaction?

* Do they agree or disagree with your ideas?

* Can you come to a compromise?

ACTIVITY

Compare and Contrast the Declaration of Sentiments

The Declaration of Sentiments was modeled after the Declaration of Independence. In this activity, you will explore how Elizabeth Cady Stanton took the ideas and beliefs in the Declaration of Independence and used it for a different purpose.

Read the first two paragraphs of the Declaration of Sentiments. Then read the first two paragraphs of the Declaration of Independence. You can find the texts here.

Declaration of Sentiments Fordham 🔎

Declaration of Independence 🔎

Set up a chart to compare the two documents. How are they the same? How are they different?

Read the next section in the Declaration of Sentiments, the list of complaints or sentiments against American men in 1848. Pick five of these sentiments. What did the writers mean? Rewrite these sentiments in everyday English that is easy for family and friends to understand.

The next section in the Declaration of Sentiments lists resolutions or things that the people at the conference wanted done. What would you add to this list? What would you take off?

EXPLORE MORE: Imagine that you lived in 1848 and read the Declaration of Sentiments. Do you agree with it or disagree with it? Write a newspaper editorial supporting or opposing the Declaration of Sentiments.

ACTIVITY

Choose a Side:
Federalist vs. Anti-Federalist

The idea of whether states or the central government should have more power played a pivotal role in developing the U.S. Constitution. Federalists wanted a strong central government. They believed that this was the best way to protect the country. Anti-federalists did not support a strong central government and instead wanted power to remain with the states. They feared that a strong central government would not protect the basic rights and freedoms of its citizens. In this activity, you will consider the pros and cons of each position and then choose a side!

DID YOU KNOW?

James Madison, one of the authors of the Federalist Papers, became the fourth president of the United States.

Consider the benefits and drawbacks of the federalist and anti-federalist viewpoints. Create a list of arguments for each side in your history notebook.

If you had been a colonist in 1787, which side would you have supported? Why would you have chosen this side?

Write a persuasive essay supporting the side you choose. Explain the reasons you chose this viewpoint.

EXPLORE MORE: Create a counterpoint argument to your essay. How would you counter each point made? Write a short speech to deliver your response.

A Slave's Diary

Lincoln's Emancipation Proclamation announced that all slaves in the Confederate states were free. His proclamation brought hope for freedom and the possibility of a new future to millions of Southern slaves. What might that have felt like for people living at the time?

Imagine that you are a slave living in one of the Southern states in 1862. You have heard whispers about the Emancipation Proclamation and the promise that President Abraham Lincoln has made to free the slaves in your community.

Write a diary entry from the perspective of a person living in slavery. Be sure to include your emotions at the time as well as your plans for the future.

A Slave's Story in His Own Words

William Quinn was born into slavery on a farm in Kentucky. Around the age of 10, Quinn was emancipated by the farm's owner, Steve Stone, a full year before Lincoln's Emancipation Proclamation. Treated well by his owner, Quinn describes what he did after being freed:

"After emancipation we stayed with the Stone family for some time, 'cause they were good to us and we had no place to go."

You can read the rest of Quinn's account of slavery here. How would you have reacted to being emancipated? How would your decision be different if conditions were different where you lived?

born in slavery federal writers project quinn 🔍

ACTIVITY

Martin Luther King Jr. and the Declaration of Independence

On August 28, 1963, legendary civil rights activist Dr. Martin Luther King Jr. spoke on the steps of the Lincoln Memorial during the March on Washington for Jobs and Freedom. His electrifying speech was a defining moment for the Civil Rights Movement. How was Dr. King's speech influenced by a document written nearly two centuries earlier, the Declaration of Independence?

Read a transcript of Dr. King's "I Have a Dream" speech. You can find it online here.

King I have dream speech archives 🔍

What rights does Dr. King claim for African Americans?

What parts of Dr. King's speech show ideas from the Declaration of Independence?

Create a chart that compares an element of the speech to something in the Declaration of Independence.

How was Dr. King influenced by the Declaration of Independence?

EXPLORE MORE: What other events, speeches, and documents in American history were influenced by the Declaration of Independence? Create a timeline showing these documents and events.

Chapter 5

Magna Carta
1215

English Bill
of Rights
1689

ENGLAND

Declaration of the Rights of
Man and of the Citizen
1789

Universal
Declaration of
Human Rights
1948

FRANCE

IMPORTANT DOCUMENTS OF OTHER NATIONS

Around the world, documents have played an important role in the history of people and government. Documents such as Magna Carta (1215) and the English Bill of Rights (1689) paved the way for America's founding documents. The French Rights of Man (1789) and the United Nation's Universal Declaration of Human Rights (1948) were influenced and inspired by the American charters.

Before writing the Declaration of Independence, America's Founding Fathers looked to the past for examples of people asserting their rights. They found it in Great Britain's Magna Carta. Magna Carta established for the first time the idea that everyone, including the king, must follow the law.

? ESSENTIAL QUESTION

How do documents from around the world reflect the basic values of all people?

～～～ MAGNA CARTA (1215) ～～～

Magna Carta was originally written as a peace treaty between King John of England and his rebellious barons. Magna Carta means "The Great Charter."

On the plains of Runnymede, England, a group of about 40 barons confronted King John in 1215. The king needed cash to pay for his war with France and he had demanded a fee from the barons who had not joined his war. The barons protested the fee and condemned his policies. They confronted the king in Runnymede and demanded he recognize certain traditional rights.

The barons insisted these rights be written down and confirmed with the king's royal seal. To avoid a civil war, the king agreed, and the resulting document was Magna Carta.

When writing Magna Carta, the barons never intended to protect the rights of an entire country. Instead, they were narrowly focused on protecting the rights and property of themselves and the few powerful families they represented. The barons wanted to force the king to recognize their liberties and to limit his ability to tax them to raise money. In Magna Carta, they also reasserted the idea of "due process," which is the legal requirement for the state to respect all legal rights owed to a person.

fundamental: something that is of central importance.

nullify: to make legally void or to cancel out.

peer: an equal or someone like you.

WORDS TO KNOW

Most of the clauses granted by the king related to specific complaints the barons had with the way he ruled them. However, there were some **fundamental** values that would last for centuries. One wording change in the final document proved to be very important to future generations of British people. The term "any baron" in the original draft was eventually replaced with "any freeman" in the final draft. Using the word "freeman" allowed the document to include all English people in future years.

Only 10 weeks after King John signed Magna Carta, Pope Innocent III **nullified** the document, saying that the king had been forced into agreeing to it. England fell into civil war, which ended only with King John's death the following year, in October 1216.

DID YOU KNOW?

When Magna Carta was reissued and confirmed, copies of the document were sent to the counties so that everyone would know their rights.

Although Magna Carta failed as a peace treaty between the king and his barons, it provided a new framework for the relationship between a king and his subjects. After King John's death, Magna Carta was reissued several times. The original Magna Carta contained 63 clauses. Today, only three clauses remain part of English law. One defends the liberties and rights of the English Church. The other guarantees the liberties and customs of London and other towns. The third is the most famous, stating:

*"No free man shall be seized or imprisoned, or stripped of his rights or possessions, or outlawed or exiled, or deprived of his standing in any other way, nor will we proceed with force against him, or send others to do so, except by the lawful judgement of his **peers** or by the law of the land. To no one will we sell, to no one deny or delay right or justice."*

Magna Carta

From a translation of the 1297 version of Magna Carta:

"In the first place we grant to God and confirm by this our present charter for ourselves and our heirs in perpetuity that the English Church is to be free and to have all its rights fully and its liberties entirely. We furthermore grant and give to all the freemen of our realm for ourselves and our heirs in perpetuity the liberties written below to have and to hold to them and their heirs from us and our heirs in perpetuity."

Read the full document here. Is the language similar to other documents you've studied in this book? How is it different?

Magna Carta archives 🔍

This clause granted all free men the right to justice and a fair trial. In 1215, there were very few free men in England. The majority of people were peasants who lived on and farmed land owned by the lord. However, future generations of people interpreted this clause for their own ideas and purposes. In the fourteenth century, Parliament said this clause guaranteed trial by jury. In the seventeenth century, Sir Edward Coke, a leader in Parliament and a prominent judge, said the clause meant even the king was not above the law. This clause became the basis for similar rights in the American Bill of Rights (1791) and the Universal Declaration of Human Rights (1948).

During the American Revolution, the colonists looked to Magna Carta to justify their actions. They believed that they were due the same rights as English citizens, and that these rights had been guaranteed to them in Magna Carta. Using Magna Carta as a guide, they wrote state constitutions and later the U.S. Constitution and Bill of Rights.

abdicate: to give up or renounce an office.

constitutional monarchy: a form of government where a king or queen acts as head of state, but the law limits and defines the ruler's powers.

parliamentary system: a representative democracy in which the majority party in the legislative parliament passes laws unchecked. The leader of the majority party serves as prime minister, the executive.

WORDS TO KNOW

In 1215, when King John placed his seal on Magna Carta, he acknowledged the concept that no man, not even a king, is above the law. This concept has lasted for centuries. Magna Carta stood as a defense against tyranny in England. It also became a symbol for individual rights. These ideas had a direct impact on the U.S. Constitution and Bill of Rights, which protect the individual freedoms of Americans.

ENGLISH BILL OF RIGHTS (1689)

In 1688, the people of England and Scotland rebelled against King James II in the Glorious Revolution. They were upset that the king did not let them vote or practice the religion of their choice. They invited William of Orange to take over as king. A Dutch leader, William was married to Mary, the daughter of King James II. When William's army marched toward London, King James II **abdicated** the throne and fled England. Parliament insisted that William and Mary accept the English Bill of Rights before they were recognized as the new king and queen.

The English Bill of Rights was an act passed by Parliament in 1689. It guaranteed the rights of citizens of England and protected them from the crown. The Bill of Rights created a **constitutional monarchy** in England. In this form of government, a monarch acts as the head of state, but in a mostly ceremonial position. Constitutional monarchies use a **parliamentary system**, with a prime minister as the head of the government.

The Rights of an Englishman

The English Bill of Rights included several provisions, as well as a list of the misdeeds of King James II. In 13 articles, it confirmed the rights of Parliament and the people, while also placing limits on the crown's power. The bill stated that all Englishmen had certain civil and political rights, which include the following freedoms.

> freedom from royal interference with the law

> freedom from taxation by royal prerogative, without agreement by Parliament

> freedom from a peacetime standing army, without agreement by Parliament

> freedom to have arms for defense, as allowed by law

> freedom to petition the king

> freedom to elect members of Parliament without interference from the sovereign

> the freedom of speech in Parliament

> freedom from cruel and unusual punishments and excessive bail

> freedom from fines and forfeitures without trial

The English Bill of Rights established that the king or queen could not rule without the consent of Parliament. It put in place a constitutional form of government. Under this form of government, rights and liberties of the citizens were protected by English law. A century later, the English Bill of Rights served as a great influence on the American colonies and the American Bill of Rights.

The English Bill of Rights and Magna Carta are two significant historical documents that outline the relationship between the English monarchy and its people. Magna Carta took the first steps in establishing a democratic basis for England by limiting the powers of the king. It established the idea of due process of law and prevented the king from taking property or creating new taxes without the consent of Parliament.

aristocracy: a hereditary ruling, elite class of people.

WORDS TO KNOW

The 1689 English Bill of Rights took the democratic process even further by guaranteeing free elections and frequent meetings of Parliament. It gave the English people the right of free speech to complain to the crown in Parliament. It also established a representative government that makes the laws for the people.

English Bill of Rights (1689)

In this portion of the English Bill of Rights, the document lists 13 rights of the people and Parliament. Here are a few of them.

"And thereupon the said Lords Spiritual and Temporal and Commons, pursuant to their respective letters and elections, being now assembled in a full and free representative of this nation, taking into their most serious consideration the best means for attaining the ends aforesaid, do in the first place (as their ancestors in like case have usually done) for the vindicating and asserting their ancient rights and liberties declare

That the pretended power of suspending the laws or the execution of laws by regal authority without consent of Parliament is illegal;

That the pretended power of dispensing with laws or the execution of laws by regal authority, as it hath been assumed and exercised of late, is illegal;

That the commission for erecting the late Court of Commissioners for Ecclesiastical Causes, and all other commissions and courts of like nature, are illegal and pernicious;

That levying money for or to the use of the Crown by pretence of prerogative, without grant of Parliament, for longer time, or in other manner than the same is or shall be granted, is illegal."

You can read the full document online at this website. What do you find that is similar to the U.S. Constitution and Bill of Rights?

English Bill of Rights Yale 🔍

A century later in America, the colonists expected to have these same rights. When they believed that the actions of King George III denied them the basic rights guaranteed by Magna Carta and the English Bill or Rights, the seeds of the American Revolution took root. Many of the themes found in Magna Carta and the 1689 English Bill of Rights can be found in the Declaration of Independence, the U.S. Constitution, and the American Bill of Rights.

DID YOU KNOW? ★ ★ ★
The full name of the English Bill of Rights is "An Act Declaring the Rights and Liberties of the Subject and Settling the Succession of the Crown."

FRENCH DECLARATION OF THE RIGHTS OF ～ MAN AND OF THE CITIZEN (1789) ～

In the 1780s, the French people were fed up with their rulers. They had suffered through years of expensive wars, bad harvests, class tensions, unemployment, food shortages, and overpopulation. At the same time, the nobles lived pampered and lavish lives. Like the American colonists, the French thought their rulers treated them unfairly. Certain rights and freedoms were given only to nobles and members of the **aristocracy**, not the common people.

In 1789, King Louis XVI called for an assembly of the Estates General. This was the legislative body in France at the time. It was made up of three groups representing the nobles, the clergy, and the commoners. The commoners were tired of the conditions in France. They wanted change and pushed for reforms.

When the king barred them from the assembly, they banded together and formed the National Constituent Assembly. They swore to not disband until France had a new constitution. At the same time, public unrest spilled into Paris. On July 14, 1789, mobs stormed Paris's Bastille prison.

DID YOU KNOW?

Thomas Jefferson helped the Marquis de Lafayette edit an early draft of the Declaration of the Rights of Man and of the Citizen.

The citizens of Paris moved into open rebellion and began executing members of the nobility.

A Violent Revolution

The French Revolution quickly became violent. One of its leaders, Maximilien Robespierre, became a cruel and absolute ruler. Robespierre was a popular lawyer and member of the National Assembly. He aligned with radical revolutionaries. He became very powerful and led France between 1793 and 1794.

Robespierre wanted to create an ideal society and was ruthless in his efforts to do so. He created a state religion and revoked rights to property and legal defense. He called for the execution of anyone labeled an enemy of the revolution. In his own way, Robespierre created a government that was just as oppressive as the monarchy he had helped to overthrow. Eventually, the French grew tired of his methods. He was arrested, tried, and executed in 1794.

During the rebellion, the National Constituent Assembly moved to establish the rights of the French people, especially the commoners. The members looked to the American Declaration of Independence as a model. On August 26, 1789, the assembly issued the Declaration of the Rights of Man and of the Citizen. It was drafted by the Marquis de Lafayette, who had served under General George Washington in the American Revolution.

French Declaration of the Rights of Man and of the Citizen

The translated text for the French Declaration of the Rights of Man and of the Citizen can be found here. What evidence do you see of the influence of the American Declaration of Independence?

Rights of Man and Citizen Yale 🔍

The Declaration of the Rights of Man and of the Citizen stated the basic rights of human beings. It listed the limits of the government. Some of its articles are listed here.

• Men are born and remain free and equal in rights (Article 1).

• The purpose of all political association is the preservation of the natural . . . rights of man. These rights are liberty, property, security, and resistance to oppression (Article 2).

• Liberty consists in the ability to do whatever does not harm another (Article 4).

• No one should be disturbed for his opinions, even in religion, provided that their manifestation does not trouble public order as established by law (Article 10).

• The free communication of thoughts and opinions is one of the most precious of the rights of man. Every citizen may therefore speak, write, and print freely . . . (Article 11).

DID YOU KNOW?
The Declaration of the Rights of Man was not itself law, but its principles formed the basis of the future French constitution and law.

In September 1791, the National Constituent Assembly presented a new constitution, one that created a constitutional monarchy for France. Louis XVI was still the king, but he no longer had absolute power. Instead, as a constitutional monarch, his power came from the law and the legislature. He was required to cooperate with the new Legislative Assembly.

The new constitution also defined voting rights. Only male residents of France who were more than 25 years old and paid taxes had the right to vote. While this provision expanded voting rights, it still denied the vote to most of France's common people.

UNIVERSAL DECLARATION
OF HUMAN RIGHTS

Almost two centuries after the U.S. Constitution and the Bill of Rights were written and adopted, the United Nations General Assembly issued a milestone document in the history of human rights. Drafted in response to World War II, the Universal Declaration of Human Rights (UDHR) lists, for the first time, the fundamental human rights that are to be universally protected. Following its issuance, the United Nations called upon all member countries to publicize the UDHR so that it could be shared, displayed, read, and discussed in schools and other educational institutions around the world.

The horrors of World War II, in particular the **genocides** committed by Nazi Germany, stunned the world. The international community agreed that war could no longer be used as an excuse to commit crimes against humans.

For the first time in history, the international community agreed that serious violations of human rights should not be tolerated. They acknowledged that protecting human rights was not the responsibility of only a single country, but was the responsibility of the entire world.

PS

Universal Declaration of Human Rights

You can read the document here. Is there anything you would add to or subtract from this document if you were helping to draft it?

Universal Declaration Human Rights 🔎

inalienable: something that can't be given away or taken away.

indivisible: something that cannot be separated or divided into parts.

WORDS TO KNOW

The United Nations decided that a strong and unified declaration against human rights violations was needed to prevent future violations. So the organization appointed a commission to draft a document that listed universally recognized rights and freedoms.

The Commission on Human Rights, led by American Eleanor Roosevelt, got to work. The members of the commission knew that they needed to create a document that all countries could adopt. The ideas it contained needed to be universal and work for different religions, cultures, and governments.

The document they drafted became the UDHR. It is divided into two sections—the preamble and 30 articles, which list the basic rights of all humans. In Article I, the UDHR states that:

"All human beings are born free and equal in dignity and rights. They are endowed with reason and conscience and should act towards one another in a spirit of brotherhood."

DID YOU KNOW?

Although the UDHR is not a legally binding document, it has become a standard for countries around the world to follow.

Human Rights Day

The world observes Human Rights Day on December 10 to honor the day in 1948 the U.N. General Assembly adopted the UDHR. Events, exhibitions, political conferences, and meetings focus on human rights issues. Many governmental and human rights organizations schedule special events. The Nobel Peace Prize and the United Nations Prize in the Field of Human Rights are traditionally awarded on Human Rights Day.

In Article 2, the UDHR applies the document to every human on earth. It states that:

"Everyone is entitled to all the rights and freedoms set forth in this Declaration, without distinction of any kind, such as race, colour, sex, language, religion, political or other opinion, national or social origin, property, birth or other status. Furthermore, no distinction shall be made on the basis of the political, jurisdictional or international status of the country or territory to which a person belongs, whether it be independent, trust, non-self-governing or under any other limitation of sovereignty."

The UDHR is based on three key ideas. Human rights are **inalienable**, which means that no one can take them away. Human rights are also **indivisible**, which means a person cannot be granted some rights and denied others. And human rights are interdependent, connected, and working together as part of a larger framework that allows us to live safe, free, and productive lives.

The United Nations adopted the UDHR on December 10, 1948, in Paris. It states the basic principles and ideals for human rights worldwide.

ESSENTIAL QUESTION

Now it's time to consider and discuss the Essential Question: How do documents from around the world reflect the basic values of all people?

Compare the Bill of Rights: England vs. America

Written a century before the American Bill of Rights, the English Bill of Rights provided a template for future documents. By comparing the two documents, we can see how the American writers used the English model to draft their own document.

Read both the English and the American versions of the Bill of Rights. You can read them here.

English Bill of Rights 🔍   U.S. Bill of Rights 🔍

Compare the rights listed in each.

* How are they similar?

* How are they different?

* What rights did the Americans take from the English document and include in their own?

* How else did the English document influence the Americans?

Make a presentation of your research. You can use a chart, a Venn diagram, or something else. Present your findings to an audience.

EXPLORE MORE: What other events, speeches, and documents were influenced by the English Bill of Rights in world history? Create a timeline showing these documents and events.

Human Rights in the News

The UDHR states that certain fundamental human rights are universally protected. By searching through a recent newspaper, we can see how human rights are enjoyed and protected, and sometimes still violated, decades after this document was adopted.

Search through several newspapers and magazines to find articles, editorials, advertisements, and other features that deal with human rights.

Find one example for each of the following categories. For each example, what specific rights are involved?

* Rights being practiced or enjoyed
* Rights being protected
* Rights being denied
* Rights in conflict

Review the Universal Declaration of Human Rights here. What article(s) cover the rights that you found? Explain.

Universal Declaration of Human Rights 🔍

Create a poster, PowerPoint, or other type of presentation for the information that you found.

EXPLORE MORE: Take one of the human rights stories that you found and compare coverage of it in different news media—different newspapers, magazines, radio, and television programs. What differences do you notice? Why do you think coverage of the same story can vary by media source?

Bringing Human Rights to Life

Drafted in response to World War II, the UDHR listed, for the first time, the fundamental human rights that are to be universally protected. In this activity, we will work to bring a part of this document to life through a skit.

Read the UDHR. You can see a copy of it here.

Universal Declaration of Human Rights 🔍

Select an article that discusses rights that are important to you.

Create a short skit to bring this article to life. How will you illustrate the ideas in the article you have chosen?

Perform your skit for classmates, friends, and family. See if they can guess what rights you are trying to bring to life.

EXPLORE MORE: Can you think of works of fiction that portray different issues about human rights? Have you seen movies, read books, or listened to music that highlight a struggle for human rights? How is the impact of fiction different from the impact of nonfiction? Why are both genres valuable?

THE LAW

Chapter 6

THE FUTURE OF DEMOCRACY

Since its introduction in 1787, the U.S. Constitution has served as a model of democracy for many other nations around the world.

Many people consider it to be the first written constitution for a nation. Other countries have borrowed this idea of a written constitution. Many countries have also embraced ideas from the U.S. Constitution, including federalism, separation of powers, and the recognition of individual rights. The influence of the U.S. Constitution appears in the similar phrasing and borrowed passages that appear in other constitutions.

? ESSENTIAL QUESTION

How has technology caused the political process to change?

In Europe, leaders have looked to the U.S. Constitution when designing their own documents. In France, the Marquis de Lafayette consulted with Thomas Jefferson as he wrote the 1789 French Declaration of the Rights of Man and of the Citizen. Poland's Constitution, adopted in May 1791, begins with a preamble that follows the American model.

Other countries across Europe, South America, Latin America, Africa, and Asia have also turned to the U.S. Constitution when preparing their own documents. Venezuela and Argentina practice federalism, while Mexico adopted an American-style constitution in 1917. Its structure and language closely model the U.S. Constitution.

DECLINING INFLUENCE?

In the future, the influence of the Constitution on other countries as they write new constitutions might not be as strong. In fact, this decline may already be happening. In 2012, researchers from Washington University in St. Louis and the University of Virginia announced that the U.S. Constitution might be losing its appeal as a model for future constitutions. They studied the provisions of more than 700 constitutions adopted by 188 countries between 1946 and 2006. Beginning in the 1980s and 1990s, they found that the newer constitutions were less similar to the American model than in previous years.

Researchers believe the influence of the U.S. Constitution may be declining because the rights it guarantees are not the same as those that are the most popular worldwide right now. For example, the U.S. Constitution recognizes the right to a speedy and public trial, which is not a widely protected priority in other countries. Additionally, only 2 percent of the world's constitutions protect the right to bear arms.

DID YOU KNOW?

Many feel that a parliamentary system makes it easier to get things done and provides more accountability. In the U.S. system, power and control are more distributed, so the majority and minority can each blame the other for gridlock and other failures.

The U.S. Constitution fails to protect the right to travel and the right to have adequate food, education, and health care, which are issues growing in importance in the global community. Why are some rights important to people in other countries and not as important in the United States?

～ TECHNOLOGY AND DEMOCRACY ～

New technologies, such as computers, cell phones, and the Internet, have changed the way we live our lives. They can also have a big effect on democracy. Some people say that these technologies could be the biggest change in the political process since the American Revolution!

With an Internet connection, ordinary people can become more active in democracy.

They can go online to read news about the government and interviews with elected officials. They can watch online videos of speeches and debates. Special political blogs and websites have emerged to cover politics and the government all day, every day.

rally: a meeting of a large group of people to make a political protest or show support for a cause.

WORDS TO KNOW

The spread of information over the Internet is lightning fast. Rather than waiting days or weeks for newspaper coverage about events in Congress or at the White House, people can go online for instant updates on the news and issues that matter to them. Search engines allow people to easily search for information that interests them. Social media, blogs, video, email, and text alerts provide information about government activities.

Before the Internet, people talked about their political opinions with close friends, family, and coworkers. If they wanted to speak out on an issue, they had to write an opinion article for the local newspaper or send a letter to the newspaper's editor and hope it was published. Today, anyone can write a blog, post a comment, and participate in a forum. Everyday citizens can upload their own content to the Internet. People can share their views about the government and democratic issues with the rest of the country and the world. What section of the Bill of Rights protects this activity?

REACHING THE PEOPLE VIRTUALLY

Political candidates also use the Internet to reach potential voters. Email lists allow candidates to reach millions of supporters with the click of a button. Candidates also use social media sites such as Twitter, Facebook, and Instagram to post pictures and give updates about their activities and views on issues.

Mobile Access

With smartphones, people can participate in democracy at any time, from any place. Using a smartphone, an everyday citizen can read news, send tweets, or upload comments to a political blog. They can film a political **rally** with their phone's camera and upload it to social media for millions to see within seconds.

In 2008, Barack Obama announced via Twitter that he had chosen Joe Biden to be his vice presidential running mate.

Online funding efforts help candidates raise money over the Internet. The Internet has even helped officials recruit volunteers. In 2008, President Obama recruited 1.5 million volunteers for his presidential campaign online.

Once elected, government officials use social media to keep the people up to date on policies and actions. The White House uses Twitter, Facebook, Google+, LinkedIn, YouTube, and Reddit to connect with the people. Politicians have also created online videos, Q&A sessions, live streaming debates, and other online appearances. The White House even has its own YouTube channel, where the president connects directly with Americans. The channel shares behind-the-scenes video of the White House, along with interviews and videos of speeches and other events.

CHANGING ACTIVISM

The Internet has become a powerful new tool for political protest. Activists can schedule meetings, rallies, and fundraisers on social networking sites. Imagine the Founding Fathers scheduling the Constitutional Convention on Facebook or Twitter!

Protests can even take place online, often through social media sites. The Internet allows activists to carry out activities faster, cheaper, and on a larger scale. E-petitions can be signed more quickly and by more people. Ordinary people can become activists without a formal organization. Beginning in 2011, the Occupy Movement protested social and economic inequalities around the world. People in different cities used the Internet and social media to plan and organize the protests.

From the earliest days of the United States, the Founding Fathers believed in democracy and their system of government, which protected the rights and liberties of its citizens. If proven successful, they hoped their experiment in government would spread to countries around the world.

The U.S. Constitution has served as a model and inspiration for others in the cause of freedom and a government based on rule by the people.

In the years following the Declaration of Independence, movements to declare and protect the basic rights of citizens in France, Belgium, Poland, Norway, Venezuela, Mexico, and other countries relied on the United States model of government, as well as its founding documents for inspiration. Many nations adopted written constitutions as they changed their governments. In 1900, there were only about 10 democracies around the world. Today, there are more than 100 democracies worldwide, and most of them have written constitutions.

? ESSENTIAL QUESTION

Now it's time to consider and discuss the Essential Question: How has technology caused the political process to change?

Founding Fathers on Twitter

Today, many politicians use social media to quickly reach the public and talk about their positions on various issues. Imagine that Twitter existed in the 1700s. How would the Founding Fathers have used it?

NOTE: You must have an adult's permission to use social media.

With an adult's permission, go on Twitter from your computer (twitter.com). Choose the Twitter account of your favorite leader, such as the president or maybe a senator or representative from your state.

* What type of tweets do they send out?

* How are they using Twitter to further their message to the people?

* How might they deliver this kind of message if they weren't on social media?

Now imagine that you are one of the Founding Fathers. It is 1787, and the debate over the Constitution is intense.

* Create a series of at least 10 tweets that you would send to convince the people to vote for ratification. Remember—you can only use 140 characters in each tweet! Write the tweets in your history journal.

* Compose tweets from the point of view of an anti-federalist who objects to the constitution.

* Consider how debate is both limited and expanded by the use of Twitter.

DID YOU KNOW?

New technologies and tools can help more people have a voice in the democratic process than ever before.

EXPLORE MORE: Which two Founding Fathers would be most likely to get into a Twitter war? Why? Design a series of tweets between them.

Organize the Boston Tea Party on Social Media

In 1773, England's Parliament gave the East India Company a **monopoly** on tea imports to America. The colonists were required to pay a tax, called a duty, on all imported tea. By paying the duty tax, they would be acknowledging Parliament's right to tax them. Because tea was enjoyed by many throughout the colonies, Parliament assumed that the colonists would rather pay the tax than give up their tea.

When three ships loaded with tea arrived in Boston, a furious reaction erupted. On December 17, 1773, citizens tried to force the ships to leave without paying the duty tax. The collector of customs refused. Later that night, a group of about 200 men gathered near the harbor. Many of the men were members of the Sons of Liberty, a secret society formed to fight for the colonists' rights. Some were disguised as Native Americans. They marched to the wharf, boarded the ships, and dumped the tea into Boston Harbor.

What if social media existed in 1773. How might protesters have used social media to organize the Boston Tea Party?

WORDS TO KNOW

monopoly: when one company or person or group has complete control over trade of an area or product.

authoritarian: favoring complete obedience to authority instead of individual freedoms.

NOTE: You must have an adult's permission to use social media.

Imagine that you are a member of the Sons of Liberty. You want to protest the tax on tea and are angry about the ships of tea sitting in Boston Harbor. Design a protest using social media.

* What sites will you use—Facebook, Twitter, Instagram?
* What messages and images will you put on social media to organize the protest?
* How will you keep the British from discovering your plans?

EXPLORE MORE: In the age of social media, everything online lives forever. If social media existed in 1773, how could this come back to hurt the colonists who participated in the Boston Tea Party?

Technology Helps Other Governments, Too

In some cases, technology has made it easier for **authoritarian** regimes to suppress the people. For example, a 2014 Internet law in Turkey requires Internet providers to store two years of data collected on a web user's activities. The providers must turn over this data to authorities when requested. In Turkey, several people have been put on trial for insulting the president in posts they made on Facebook and Twitter. In 2015, Turkish police arrested the former Miss Turkey, 26-year-old Merve Buyuksarac, because she quoted a poem on social media that insulted Turkey's President Recep Erdogan.

Technology has only just begun changing the democratic process. As new innovations and technologies emerge, how people use these tools for democracy will also change and adapt in the future.

Freedom of Speech in the Digital Age

Many Americans feel very strongly about their right to free speech. The First Amendment to the Constitution protects freedom of speech, stating:

"Congress shall make no law respecting an establishment of religion, or prohibiting the free exercise thereof; or abridging the freedom of speech, or of the press; or the right of the people peaceably to assemble, and to petition the Government for a redress of grievances."

The Digital Age is having profound affects on the issue of freedom of speech. As people embrace the Internet and social media, there has been controversy over what is acceptable to post online and what is not. Do students have the right to post anything they want about teachers and other students on Facebook or Twitter? Can they publish threats on a blog? Are these actions protected by the First Amendment? Now, it's time for you to decide!

NOTE: You must have an adult's permission to use social media.

DID YOU KNOW?

Twitter can be a good way to get a message to lots of people at the same time, but politicians, like anyone, can get into trouble by tweeting messages they haven't thought through.

Consider the following scenarios.

* A student creates a fake Facebook profile for a teacher that describes the teacher as someone who swears a lot and complains about students.

* Angry about a test grade, a student goes home and posts an angry rant in the comment section on a teacher's website.

* A student sends threatening messages to a classmate over Twitter and posts mean comments about the student on the school's chat room.

* A group of friends create a "who's hot/who's not" list for the people in their class and post it online. Some students read it and are upset that they are listed.

ACTIVITY

The First Amendment in the Constitution protects freedom of speech. What types of speech does it protect? What types of speech are not protected by the First Amendment? Pick one of the scenarios above. Consider the following questions:

* How does their speech affect the other people in the scenario?

* Where do you draw the line in the free speech issue?

* What rights, if any, are being violated?

* What consequences, if any, should there be for crossing this line?

Do you believe that students have the right to publish anything they want online? Write a persuasive essay supporting your opinion. How would you balance the right to free speech and the digital age?

EXPLORE MORE: The right to privacy has also come under attack in the Digital Age. Computers, web cams, and smartphones can post personal details, locations, and photos in seconds. Identify which part of the Constitution protects privacy rights. What if a student posts an unflattering picture of another student online? How would you balance one student's right to free speech with the another's right to privacy?

Magna Carta in the Digital Age

To celebrate the 800th anniversary of Magna Carta in 2015, the British Museum invited young people around the world to submit a clause to update Magna Carta for the digital age. In addition, they created a webpage where visitors can read and vote for clauses they support. You can vote on the clauses and participate in building an Internet bill of rights here.

my digital rights 🔍

abdicate: to give up or renounce an office.

abolish: to put an end to a practice.

abolitionist: someone who believed that slavery should be abolished, or ended.

activist: someone who works for social or political change.

amendment: a change or addition to a document.

anarchy: a society without a government.

anti-federalist: a person who supports strong state governments instead of a central government.

aristocracy: a hereditary ruling, elite class of people.

authoritarian: favoring complete obedience to authority instead of individual freedoms.

authority: the power or right to give orders, make decisions, and enforce the laws.

autocracy: a form of government in which one person possesses unlimited power.

baron: a title of a member of the nobility.

BCE: put after a date, BCE stands for Before Common Era and counts down to zero. CE stands for Common Era and counts up from zero. These nonreligious terms correspond to BC and AD. This book was printed in 2016 CE.

bi-cameral: a legislature with two houses.

blockade: the sealing off of a place to prevent people and goods from entering or leaving.

boycott: refusing to buy or sell goods as part of a protest.

casualty: a person who is injured or killed in battle.

censor: to examine books, movies, letters, etc., in order to remove things that are considered to be offensive or harmful to society.

checks and balances: a system set up in the Constitution where each branch of the government has some authority over the others.

citizen: a person who has all the rights and responsibilities that come with being a full member of a country.

civic: relating to duty and responsibility to community.

civil right: a right that allows a person to participate fully in civil and political life without discrimination.

colony: an area that is controlled by or belongs to another country.

communist party: a political party that follows a system in which everything is owned and run by the government.

compromise: an agreement made with each side giving up something.

Confederate: the government established by the Southern slave-owning states of the United States after they left the Union in 1860 and 1861. Called the Confederate States of America or the Confederacy.

constitution: a document containing a country's basic laws and governing principles.

constitutional monarchy: a form of government where a king or queen acts as head of state, but the law limits and defines the ruler's powers.

deity: a god or goddess.

delegate: a person sent to represent others.

democracy: a system of government where the people have the ultimate power to govern themselves and determine how they will be governed.

dictatorship: a government by a dictator with absolute rule over the people.

direct democracy: a form of democracy where all citizens participate in decision making.

discrimination: to deny a group of people opportunities based on things such as race or gender.

due process: the legal requirement that the government must respect all legal rights that are owed to a person.

economic depression: a time when the economy struggles and many people lose their jobs.

elite: those viewed as the most important people.

engross: to write something in large, neat letters.

equality: having equal rights, opportunities, and status.

executive branch: the person or branch of government that enforces the law.

federalism: a division of power between the state and federal government.

federalist: a person who supports a strong central government.

fundamental: something that is of central importance.

genocide: the deliberate killing of a large group of people based on race, ethnicity, or nationality.

human rights: the rights that belong to all people, such as freedom from torture, the right to live, and freedom from slavery.

impeach: to formally charge a public official with misconduct or a crime.

inalienable: something that can't be given away or taken away.

individualism: the pursuit of personal happiness and independence rather than the goals or interests of a group.

indivisible: something that cannot be separated or divided into parts.

judicial branch: the branch of government that interprets the law.

jury: a group of people, called jurors, who hear a case in court. Jurors give their opinion, called a verdict.

justify: to show that something is right and reasonable.

legislative: having to do with the branch of government that makes or changes laws.

legislature: the lawmaking body of a government.

liberty: social and political freedoms enjoyed by people.

lottery: a random selection.

majority: a number or amount that is greater than half of the whole.

Middle Ages: the name for a period of time from around 350 to 1450 CE. It is also called the Medieval Era.

militia: a group of citizens who have been trained to fight and can be called upon when needed.

minority: a number or amount that is less than half of the whole.

mercenary: a hired soldier.

monarchy: a form of government where all power is given to a single individual, a king or queen.

monopoly: when one company or person or group has complete control over trade of an area or product.

noble: in the past, a person considered to be of the most important group in a society.

nullify: to make legally void or to cancel out.

oligarchy: government rule by a small group.

parliamentary system: a representative democracy in which the majority party in the legislative parliament passes laws unchecked. The leader of the majority party serves as prime minister, the executive.

peer: an equal or someone like you.

philosopher: a person who thinks about and questions the way things are in the world and in the universe.

polls: a survey (or count) of people's positions on issues or candidates for elected office, or a place where that survey (or count) takes place.

preamble: a brief, introductory statement.

principle: an important idea or belief that guides an individual or community.

proclamation: a public or official announcement.

Prohibition: the period of time from 1920 to 1933 when the sale of alcoholic beverages was banned—or prohibited—in the United States.

propaganda: ideas or statements that are sometimes exaggerated or even false. They are spread to help a cause, political leader, or government.

prosperity: the state of being successful and making money.

Protestant Reformation: a religious movement beginning in 1500 that rejected the Catholic pope and established the Protestant churches.

★ ★ ★ ★ ★ ★ ★ ★ ★ ★ ★   ★ ★ ★ ★ ★ ★ ★ ★ ★ ★ ★

quarter: to provide lodging and food for soldiers.

rally: a meeting of a large group of people to make a political protest or show support for a cause.

ratify: to approve formally.

reason: thinking in an orderly, sensible way.

rebel: to oppose. Rebels are people who stand up to oppose a ruler or government.

reform: a change to improve something.

representative democracy: a form of democracy where elected officials govern.

republic: a form of democracy, with elected officials.

resolution: a formal declaration of a political position or principle.

secede: to withdraw from a political alliance.

segregate: to keep people of different races, genders, or religions separate from each other.

sentiment: a view, feeling, or complaint.

sovereign: having supreme or ultimate power.

suffrage: the right to vote.

supermajority: a majority that is greater than a simple majority, such as two-thirds or three-fifths.

theocracy: government rule by religious leaders.

totalitarian: a system of government that has absolute control over its people and requires them to be completely obedient.

treason: actions that go against one's own country.

treaty: an agreement between countries or parties.

tyranny: cruel and unfair treatment by people in power.

ultimatum: a final demand.

unalienable: something that cannot be taken away or denied.

unanimous: when a group is in full agreement.

unconstitutional: not in accordance with the laws or rules of the U.S. Constitution.

veto: to reject a decision made by a legislative body.

BOOKS

Cornerstones of Freedom: The U.S. Constitution. Michael Burgan, Scholastic, 2011.

Keys to American History: Understanding Our Most Important Historic Documents. Richard Panchyk, Chicago Review Press, 2008.

The Founders: The 39 Stories Behind the U.S. Constitution. Dennis Brindell Fradin, Walker & Company, 2005.

The Great American Documents. Ruth Ashby, Farrar, Straus and Giroux, 2014.

The United States Constitution and the Bill of Rights: The Law of the Land. Anna Keegan, PowerKids Press, 2015.

Thomas Paine: Crusader for Liberty: How One Man's Ideas Helped Form a New Nation. Albert Marrin, Knopf Books for Young Readers, 2014.

Understanding the US Constitution. James Wolfe and Heather Moehn, Enslow, 2015.

We the People: The Story of Our Constitution. Lynne Cheney, Simon & Schuster, 2012.

MUSEUMS

Independence Hall, Philadelphia, Pennsylvania: *nps.gov/inde/index.htm*

National Archives Museum, Washington, DC: *archives.gov/museum*

The National Constitution Center, Philadelphia, Pennsylvania: *constitutioncenter.org*

WEBSITES

Bill of Rights Institute: *billofrightsinstitute.org*

The Charters of Freedom – The National Archives: *archives.gov/exhibits/charters*

Great American Documents: *greatamericandocuments.com*

The White House – Our Government: *whitehouse.gov/1600/executive-branch*

ESSENTIAL QUESTIONS

Introduction: How does democracy differ from other forms of government?

Chapter 1: How did the Declaration of Independence lead to the Revolutionary War?

Chapter 2: How would your life be different if the U.S. Constitution had never been written?

Chapter 3: Why is it important to be able to change the Constitution?

Chapter 4: What are some of the qualities of a document that makes a difference in history?

Chapter 5: How do documents from around the world reflect the basic values of all people?

Chapter 6: How has technology caused the political process to change?

QR CODE GLOSSARY

Page 13: mayflowerhistory. com/mayflower-compact

Page 18: archives.gov/exhibits/charters/ charters_of_freedom_zoom_pages/ charters_of_freedom_zoom_1.1.1.html

Page 21: archives.gov/exhibits/ charters/declaration_transcript.html

Page 26: archives.gov/exhibits/charters/ virginia_declaration_of_rights.html

Page 26: archives.gov/exhibits/ charters/declaration_transcript.html

Page 31: ushistory.org/paine/ commonsense/singlehtml.htm

Page 47: archives.gov/exhibits/ charters/constitution_transcript.html

Page 48: ourdocuments.gov/doc.php?f lash=true&doc=3&page=transcript

Page 48: archives.gov/exhibits/ charters/constitution_transcript.html

Page 48: billofrightsinstitute.org/ educate/educator-resources/founders

Page 50: kminot.com/html_docs/ charts/branches.html

Page 51: archives.gov/exhibits/ charters/constitution_transcript.html

Page 62: archives.gov/exhibits/charters/ constitution_amendments_11-27.html

Page 69: thomas.loc.gov/home/ histdox/fedpapers.html

Page 75: archives.gov/exhibits/featured_ documents/emancipation_proclamation

Page 80: youtube.com/ watch?v=7BEhKgoA86U

Page 82: legacy.fordham.edu/ halsall/mod/senecafalls.asp

Page 82: archives.gov/exhibits/ charters/declaration_transcript.html

Page 84: memory.loc.gov/cgi-bin/ ampage?collId=mesn&fileName=050/ mesn050.db&recNum=159&tempFile=./ temp/~ammem_kTUZ&filecode=mesn&next_ filecode=mesn&itemnum=1&ndocs=44

Page 85: archives.gov/press/ exhibits/dream-speech.pdf

Page 89: archives.gov/exhibits/featured_ documents/magna_carta/translation.html

Page 92: avalon.law.yale. edu/17th_century/england.asp

Page 95: avalon.law.yale. edu/18th_century/rightsof.asp

Page 97: un.org/en/universal- declaration-human-rights

Page 100: avalon.law.yale. edu/17th_century/england.asp

Page 100: archives.gov/exhibits/ charters/bill_of_rights_transcript.html

Page 101: un.org/en/universal- declaration-human-rights

Page 102: un.org/en/ universal-declaration-human-rights

Page 113: bl.uk/my-digital-rights/ vote-now